Cover Photo:
Currant Fruitcake 51

Adventures
in Cooking SERIES

Illustrations by Karen Rolnick

Christmas FAVORITES

Culinary Arts Institute®
A DIVISION OF DELAIR PUBLISHING COMPANY, INC.

ISBN: 0-8326-0639-1

Contents

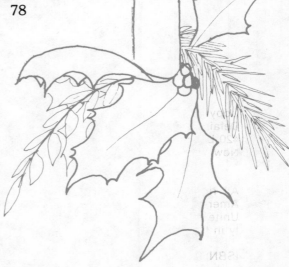

Appetizers

Cocktail Meatballs

1	large onion, minced
2	tablespoons olive oil
1½	pounds freshly ground round steak (half each of lamb and veal)
3	tablespoons cracker meal
2	cups firm-type bread, crusts removed
2	eggs
6	tablespoons chopped parsley
2	teaspoons oregano, crushed
1½	teaspoons mint
2	tablespoons vinegar
	Salt and pepper to taste
	Flour
	Olive or corn oil for deep frying heated to 365 °F

1. Brown half of onion in 2 tablespoons oil in a small frying pan. Mix with the uncooked onion and add to meat in a large bowl. Add the remaining ingredients except flour and oil. Toss lightly with two forks to mix thoroughly.

2. Dust hands with flour. Roll a small amount of meat at a time between palms, shaping into a ball.

3. To heated fat in deep fryer, add the meatballs a layer at a time. Fry until browned on all sides (about 12 minutes). Serve hot.

30 to 40 meatballs

Baked Clams Oregano

12	clams
3	tablespoons minced onion
	Salt and pepper to taste
1	teaspoon oregano
1	teaspoon minced parsley
5	tablespoons olive oil
	Juice of 1 lemon

1. Open clams. Arrange side by side in a small baking dish.

2. Combine onion, salt, pepper, oregano, parsley, olive oil, and lemon juice. Spoon on clam meat.

3. Bake at 325°F about 7 minutes, or until clams curl slightly at the edges.

3 servings

Planning Appetizers

There is no limit to the kinds of meat, poultry, fish, cheese, vegetables, and fruits that can be used. Though imagination and ingenuity are the only limiting factors in selecting appetizers, there is one rule that should be followed—*avoid repeating any food in the main part of the meal that has been used in the appetizers*. Remember that they are a part of the whole menu; select them to harmonize with the rest of the meal. Choose them for complementary flavors, for contrast of texture and color and variety of shape. Picture the serving dishes, trays, and other appointments as you plan the menu.

Pimiento-Crab Meat Strata Supreme

1   can (7½ oz. Alaska King crab meat, drained and flaked
½   cup finely chopped celery
¼   cup finely chopped onion
¾   cup mayonnaise
    Few grains cayenne pepper
12 slices white bread, crusts removed
    Butter or margarine softened
3   jars or cans (4 oz. each) whole pimientos, each pimiento cut in 2 or 3 large pieces
1   lb. Swiss cheese, shredded
5   eggs
3   cups milk
1   teaspoon salt
1/8 teaspoon pepper
¼   teaspoon dry mustard

1. Mix crab meat, celery, and onion. Blend in a mixture of the mayonnaise and cayenne pepper. Set aside.
2. Spread both sides of the bread slices with butter. Place half of the bread in one layer in a greased 3-quart shallow baking dish; reserve remainder.
3. Arrange half of the pimiento pieces over the bread, half of the crab mixture, and a third of the shredded cheese. Repeat layering using remainder of crab mixture, pimiento, and second third of the cheese. Cover with reserved bread and sprinkle with the remaining cheese.
4. Beat remaining ingredients together until frothy and blended. Pour over all. Let stand 1 hour.
5. Bake at 425°F 1 hour, or until puffed and browned.
6. Garnish top with three well-drained whole pimientos arranged in a bell cluster with green pepper strips between the bells. Nestle a small parsley bouquet at center.

6 to 8 servings

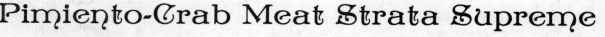

Shrimp Cocktail

1½   lbs. fresh shrimp with shells
3   cups water
3   tablespoons lemon juice
1   tablespoon salt
1   bay leaf

1. Wash shrimp in cold water.
2. Drop shrimp into a boiling mixture of water, lemon juice, salt, and bay leaf.
3. Cover tightly. Simmer 5 min. or until shrimp are pink and tender.
4. Drain shrimp and cover with cold water to chill. Drain shrimp again.
5. Remove tiny legs. Peel shells from the shrimp. Cut a slit along back (outer curved surface) of shrimp to expose the black vein. With knife point, remove vein in one piece. Rinse the shrimp quickly under running cold water. Drain them on absorbent paper. Store in refrigerator until ready to use.
6. Serve shrimp on **lettuce** or **curly endive** with **Peppy Cocktail Sauce (below)**.

About 3 cups shrimp

Hot Shrimp Appetizer: Follow recipe for Shrimp Cocktail. Arrange shrimp on broiler rack. Brush with a mixture of ½ **cup butter or margarine,** melted, and **3 tablespoons lemon juice.** Place under broiler about 2 in. from heat for 3 to 5 min., or until shrimp are thoroughly heated. Insert wooden picks. Serve immediately with **Peppy Cocktail Sauce.**

Shrimp With Peppy Cocktail Sauce

1   cup ketchup
1   tablespoon lemon juice
1   tablespoon prepared horseradish
1   teaspoon onion juice
¼   teaspoon Worcestershire sauce
    Few drops Tabasco
1   tablespoon sugar
½   teaspoon salt
1½   lbs. fresh shrimp with shells, cooked, peeled, de-veined, and chilled

1. Mix thoroughly in a small bowl all ingredients except the shrimp; refrigerate until ready to serve.
2. To prepare cocktail, line 6 chilled sherbet glasses with chilled lettuce or curly endive. Arrange about 5 shrimp in each glass and top with cocktail sauce.

6 servings

Cheese Balls

4   ounces Cheddar cheese, shredded (about 1 cup)
1   teaspoon flour
¼   teaspoon salt
    Dash pepper
1   egg white
    Oil for deep frying

1. Mix cheese, flour, salt, and pepper.
2. Beat egg white to stiff, not dry, peaks. Fold beaten egg white into cheese mixture. Form into small balls, using a rounded tablespoon of the mixture for each.
3. Heat the oil to 365°F in a wok. Fry the cheese balls, a few at a time, until brown. Serve while warm.

12 cheese balls

Cream Cheese Dainties

Apricot, Strawberry, or
Mincemeat Filling, below
½ cup butter
1 package (3 ounces) cream cheese
1 teaspoon sugar
1 cup all-purpose flour

1. Prepare desired filling or fillings and set aside.
2. Beat butter and cream cheese until well blended. Mix in sugar and then flour. Divide dough in half and chill thoroughly.
3. On a lightly floured surface, roll each half of dough to ¹⁄₁₆-inch thickness. Use floured 2-inch cookie cutters to cut about 3 dozen "bases."
4. Transfer bases to cookie sheets. Spoon about ¼ teaspoon filling in center of each cookie.
5. Cut remaining dough with the same size cutters. Use cut-out cookies or with 1-inch cutouts.
6. Bake at 375°F 6 to 8 minutes. Remove immediately to wire racks to cool.

About 5 dozen cookies

Apricot Filling: Mix ½ cup apricot preserves with ½ teaspoon lemon extract.

Strawberry Filling: Mix ½ cup strawberry preserves with ½ teaspoon almond extract.

Mincemeat Filling: Mix ½ cup prepared mincemeat with ½ teaspoon orange extract.

Note: If desired, make tart shells from dough. Roll dough to ¹⁄₁₆-inch thickness and cut out rounds with a 2¾-inch cookie cutter. Carefully line well-buttered 2¼x¾-inch tart pan wells with rounds of dough; prick with a fork. Bake at 375°F 8 to 10 minutes, or until lightly browned. Cool; remove from pans. Fill with fruit or cream filling.

About 3 dozen tart shells

Eggnog Fondue

2 eggs, beaten
2 tablespoons sugar or honey
1/8 teaspoon salt
1½ cups milk
½ teaspoon vanilla extract
3 tablespoons arrowroot
3 tablespoons dark rum
Nutmeg
Fruitcake, cut into ¾-inch pieces

1. Beat together eggs, sugar, and salt. Stir in milk and vanilla extract.
2. Pour eggnog into a nonmetal fondue pot. Mix arrowroot with 1 tablespoon rum and stir into the eggnog.
3. Cook over medium heat until mixture thickens, stirring occasionally. Stir in remaining rum.
4. Keep fondue warm while dipping fruitcake pieces.

6 to 8 servings

Soups & Salads

Shrimp Salad Duo Elegante

2 lbs. cooked shrimp, peeled and deveined
½ cup chopped pickled watermelon rind (reserve ½ cup syrup)
⅔ cup lime juice
4 teaspoons French dressing mix
2 pkgs. (3 oz. each) strawberry-flavored gelatin
1½ cups boiling water
1 can (29 oz.) pear halves, drained (reserve 1½ cups syrup)
1½ cups sliced celery
¼ cup coarsely chopped pistachio nuts
French Mayonnaise

1. Put shrimp into a large shallow dish and pour a mixture of the reserved syrup, lime juice, and French dressing mix over the shrimp; cover and marinate 2 hours, turning occasionally. Drain, reserving marinade; set shrimp aside.

2. Dissolve gelatin in boiling water; stir in 1 cup of the marinade and the reserved pear syrup; chill until gelatin is slightly thickened.

3. Pour gelatin into a 2-quart ring mold to ¼-inch depth; set remaining gelatin aside. Cut three pear halves in half lengthwise, and arrange, rounded side down, in bottom of mold; chill until gelatin is just set, but not firm.

4. Meanwhile, cut remaining pears and 2 cups of the shrimp into small pieces; add to remaining gelatin with the watermelon rind and blend well.

5. Spoon mixture over layer in mold and chill until firm, about 3 hours.

6. Combine remaining shrimp (about 2 cups) with celery, nuts, and the French Mayonnaise; toss lightly to mix. Refrigerate.

7. Unmold salad onto a chilled large serving plate and garnish mold with salad greens. Spoon shrimp mixture into the center.

8 to 10 servings

French Mayonnaise: Mix together ½ cup mayonnaise, ¼ cup clear French dressing, and ¼ teaspoon horseradish.

Red Vegetable Salad

1 **pint cherry tomatoes, stems removed, cut in half**
20 **radishes, sliced**
1 **small red onion, sliced**
3 **tablespoons wine vinegar**
2 **teaspoon salad oil**
1 **teaspoon salt**
2 **teaspoons snipped fresh mint**
1/8 **teaspoon freshly ground white pepper**
Lettuce leaves

1. Combine all ingredients except lettuce leaves in a medium bowl; refrigerate covered 2 hours, stirring occasionally.
2. Serve vegetables on lettuce.

4 to 6 servings

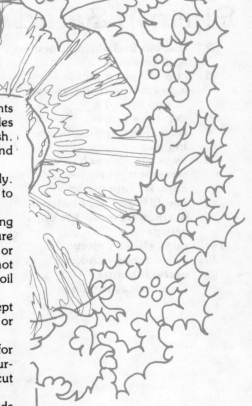

Salad Pointers

A salad is only as good as its makings so select the ingredients with care. Greens should be fresh, crisp, and dry, vegetables garden fresh, and fruits firm, fully ripe, and free from blemish. When using canned products, choose those of good quality and appearance.

Chill all salad ingredients, bowls, and plates thoroughly. With the exception of a few hot salads, coldness is essential to the appeal of all salads.

Trim and rinse greens under running cold water, handling them carefully to avoid bruising. Shake off the excess moisture and then gently pat dry before putting them into a plastic bag or the vegetable drawer and into your refrigerator. Wet greens not only make watery salads, they present a surface to which an oil dressing cannot cling.

Greens should always be broken or torn, never cut (except in the case of head lettuce which is to be served in wedges or quarters).

Tomatoes may be peeled or not, as your family prefers, for use in salads. Unpeeled tomato shells or tomato cups are sturdier and keep their shape better; peeled ones are easier to cut with a fork.

Tomato wedges or chunks should be added to tossed salads just before serving, as their juice tends to make the dressing watery.

Salade Nicoise

Salad Dressing, below
3 medium-sized cooked potatoes, sliced
1 pkg. (9 oz.) frozen green beans, cooked
1 clove garlic, cut in half
1 small head Boston lettuce
2 cans (6½ or 7 oz. each) tuna, drained
1 mild onion, quartered and thinly sliced
2 ripe tomatoes, cut in wedges
2 hard-cooked eggs, quartered
1 can (2 oz.) rolled anchovy fillets, drained
¾ cup pitted ripe olives
1 tablespoon capers

1. Pour enough salad dressing over warm potato slices and cooked beans (in separate bowls) to coat vegetables.
2. Before serving, rub the inside of a large shallow salad bowl with the cut surface of the garlic. Line the bowl or a large serving platter with the lettuce.
3. Unmold the tuna in center of bowl and separate into chunks.
4. Arrange separate mounds of the potatoes, green beans, onions, tomatoes, and hard-cooked eggs in colorful groupings around the tuna. Garnish with anchovies, olives and capers.
5. Pour dressing over all before serving.

6 to 8 Servings

Salad Dressing: Combine in a jar or bottle ½ cup olive oil or salad oil, 2 tablespoons red wine vinegar, a mixture of 1 teaspoon salt, ½ teaspoon pepper, and 1 teaspoon dry mustard, 1 tablespoon finely chopped chives, and 1 tablespoon finely chopped parsley. Shake vigorously to blend well before pouring over salad.

About ⅔ Cup

Crab Meat Salad

Cooked Pineapple Salad Dressing, page 100
2 cups boiling water
2 pkgs. (3 oz. each) lemon-flavored gelatin
½ teaspoon salt
1 cup cold water
3 tablespoons cider vinegar
¼ cup large-curd creamed cottage cheese, sieved
½ cup coarsely chopped salted almonds
½ cup finely chopped celery
¼ cup finely chopped green pepper
1 tablespoon grated onion
2 teaspoons chopped pimiento
¾ lb. fresh crab meat, separated in pieces (bony tissue removed)
½ cup chilled heavy cream, whipped
Fresh pineapple, thinly sliced pieces

1. Prepare salad dressing; chill thoroughly.
2. Pour boiling water over gelatin and salt in a bowl; stir until gelatin is dissolved. Blend in the cold water and vinegar. Chill until mixture is slightly thickened.
3. Thoroughly mix cottage cheese, almonds, celery, green pepper, onion, and pimiento with ½ cup of the salad dressing. Gently blend in crab meat.
4. Stir the crab meat mixture into slightly thickened gelatin. Turn into a 2-quart fancy mold and chill until firm.
5. Fold the whipped cream into the remaining salad dressing. Chill until ready to serve.
6. Unmold salad onto chilled serving plate and surround mold with the chilled sliced pineapple. Serve with the salad dressing.

About 8 servings

Breads

Christmas Bread

2	envelopes active dry yeast
2	cups scalded milk, cooled to 105° to 115°F
1	cup sugar
1	teaspoon salt
4	eggs (or 8 yolks), well beaten
½	cup unsalted butter, melted
7½	to 8 cups all-purpose flour
1½	teaspoons cardamom, pounded, or 1 teaspoon mastic
½	cup dried golden currants
¾	cup chopped walnuts
2	egg whites, beaten
4	tablespoons sugar

1. Sprinkle yeast over 1 cup warm milk in a small bowl; stir until dissolved. Set aside.
2. Reserve 2 teaspoons sugar for pounding with mastic, if using. Put sugar into a bowl and add salt, eggs, remaining 1 cup milk, and butter; mix well.
3. Put 7 cups flour into a large bowl. Stir in cadamon, or pound mastic with 2 tablespoons sugar (so it will not become gummy) and add. Make a well and add dissolved yeast, egg mixture, currants, and nuts; mix well.
4. Knead dough on a floured board, adding the remaining 1 cup flour as required. Knead dough until smooth (5 to 6 minutes).
5. Place dough in a greased bowl. Turn until surface is completely greased. Cover. Set in a warm place until double in bulk.
6. Punch dough down. Form into two round loaves and place in buttered 10-inch pans.
7. Cover and let rise again in a warm place until double in bulk.
8. Bake at 375°F 15 minutes. Remove from oven and brush with beaten egg whites, then sprinkle with sugar. Remove from oven and brush with beaten egg whites, then sprinkle with sugar. Return to oven. Turn oven control to 325°F and bake about 35 to 40 minutes, or until bread is done.

Butter Pecan Shortbread

Shortbread:

1	cup butter
½	cup firmly packed light brown sugar
2¼	cups all-purpose flour
½	cup finely chopped pecans

Decorator Icing:

2	tablespoons butter
¼	teaspoon vanilla extract
1	cup confectioners' sugar
	Milk (about 1 tablespoon)
	Red and green food coloring

1. To prepare shortbread, beat butter until softened; add brown sugar gradually, beating until fluffy. Add flour gradually, beating until well blended. Mix in pecans.
2. Chill dough until easy to handle.
3. On a lightly floured surface, pat and roll dough into a 14x10-inch rectangle about ¼ inch thick. Cut dough into 24 squares. Divide each square into 4 triangles.
4. Transfer triangles to ungreased cookie sheets.
5. Bake at 300°F 18 to 20 minutes, or until lightly browned. Remove to wire racks to cool.
6. To prepare icing, cream butter with vanilla extract in a small bowl. Add confectioners' sugar gradually, beating until blended. Blend in enough milk for desired consistency for icing. Color one third of icing red and two thirds green. Force icing through a decorator tube to make a holly decoration on each cookie.

8 dozen cookies

Fruit Bread, Milan Style

2	packages active dry yeast
¼	cup warm water
1	cup butter, melted
1	cup sugar
1	teaspoon salt
2	cups sifted all-purpose flour
½	cup milk, scalded and cooled to lukewarm
2	eggs
4	egg yolks
3½	cups all-purpose flour
1	cup dark seedless raisins
¾	cup chopped citron
½	cup all-purpose flour
1	egg, slightly beaten
1	tablespoon water

1. Dissolve yeast in the warm water.
2. Pour melted butter into large bowl of electric mixer. Add the sugar and salt gradually, beating constantly.
3. Beating thoroughly after each addition, alternately add the 2 cups flour in thirds and lukewarm milk in halves to the butter mixture. Add yeast and beat well.
4. Combine eggs and egg yolks and beat until thick and piled softly. Add the beaten eggs all at one time to yeast mixture and beat well. Beating thoroughly after each addition, gradually add the 3½ cups flour. Stir in raisins and citron.
5. Sift half of the remaining ½ cup flour over a pastry canvas or board. Turn dough onto floured surface; cover and let rest 10 minutes.
6. Sift remaining flour over dough. Pull dough from edges toward center until flour is worked in. (It will be sticky.) Put dough into a greased deep bowl and grease top of dough. Cover; let rise in a warm place (about 80°F) about 2½ hours.
7. Punch down dough and pull edges of dough in to center. Let rise again about 1 hour.
8. Divide dough into halves and shape each into a round loaf. Put each loaf into a well-greased 8-inch layer cake pan. Brush surfaces generously with a mixture of slightly beaten egg and water. Cover; let rise again about 1 hour.
9. Bake at 350°F 40 to 45 minutes, or until golden brown. Remove to wire racks to cool.

Helpful Hints About Breads

• To glaze tops of fancy breads and rolls brush before baking with slightly beaten egg white mixed with 1 tablespoon milk or water; or egg yolk slightly beaten with a little milk or water.
• To slice newly baked bread, cut with a hot knife.
• To butter bread for thin sandwiches, spread end of loaf with softened butter, then cut off a slice as thin a possible. Repeat buttering and slicing.
• To freshen rolls, place them in a heavy paper bag. Twist top of bag and place in a 400°F oven 10 to 15 minutes. (Or wrap securely in aluminum foil.)
• To prepare crumbs from dry bread, force through the fine blade of food chopper or place dry bread in a small plastic bag and crush with a rolling pin. Crush in an electric blender, if available. If using the food chopper, tie a paper bag onto end of food chopper to keep crumbs from scattering.

Coffee Bread

½ cup finely chopped blanched almonds
1 cup milk or cream
1 pkg. active dry yeast
¼ cup warm water
½ cup butter
⅓ cup sugar
1 teaspoon salt
3½ cup sifted all-purpose flour
1 egg

1. Two baking sheets will be needed.
2. Set out finely chopped blanched almonds.
3. Scald milk or cream.
4. Meanwhile, soften dry yeast in ¼ cup warm water, 105°F to 115°F (Or if using compressed yeast, soften 1 cake in ¼ cup lukewarm water, 80°F to 85°F.)
5. Set aside.
6. Put into a large bowl butter, sugar, and salt.
7. Immediately pour scalded milk over ingredients in bowl. When lukewarm, blend in 1 cup all-purpose flour beating until smooth. Stir softened yeast and add, mixing well.
8. Add about one-half the flour to the yeast mixture and beat until very smooth.
9. Beat in 1 egg, well beaten.
10. Then beat in enough remaining flour to make a soft dough. Turn dough onto a lightly floured surface and allow dough to rest 5 to 10 minutes.
11. Knead dough.
12. Form dough into a large ball and put it into a greased, deep bowl. Turn dough to bring greased surface to top. Cover with waxed paper and towel and let stand in warm place (about 80°F) until dough is doubled.
13. Punch down with fist; pull edges of dough in to center and turn dough completely over in bowl. Cover and let rise again until nearly doubled. Punch down and turn dough out onto lightly floured surface. Divide dough into two portions and shape into oblong loaves.
14. Lightly grease the baking sheets.
15. Place loaves on baking sheets and brush with egg white, slightly beaten.
16. Sprinkle each loaf with one-half of a mixture of chopped almonds and sugar.
17. Cover and let rise about 45 min., or until dough is doubled.
18. Bake at 375°F 20 to 25 min.
19. Cool completely on cooling racks.

2 loaves bread

Christmas Rolls: Follow recipe for Coffee Bread. Instead of dividing dough for loaves, break off pieces of dough and roll with hands into strips 4 in. long and ½ in. thick. Coil each end in to center of strip. Place two coiled strips together so that coils are back to back. Or place two coiled strips at right angles, one on top of the other. Or shape strip into a half circle and coil ends in opposite directions. Press **1 raisin** into the center of each coil. Place rolls on greased baking sheets. Omit egg white and almond-sugar mixture. Cover and let rise until doubled. Bake at 375°F about 15 to 20 min.

About 4 doz. rolls

Fish & Shellfish

Codfish for Christmas

1	**pound salted codfish (1 piece)**
2	**small onions, peeled**
	Salt and pepper
3	**medium (1 pound) tomatoes, peeled, seeded, and cut in pieces**
2	**cloves garlic, peeled**
3	**tablespoons oil**
5	**pickled chilies, seeded and cut in strips**
3	**canned pimentos, cut in strips**
½	**cup pimento-stuffed olives**
1	**tablespoon chopped parsley**

1. Soak codfish several hours in cold water; change water several times.
2. Drain codfish and put into a saucepan; add 1 onion and water to cover. Bring to simmering, cover, and cook gently about 15 minutes, or until fish flakes easily when tested with a fork. Drain. Season with salt and pepper.
3. Meanwhile, puree tomatoes, remaining onion (cut in quarters), and garlic in an electric blender.
4. Heat oil in a skillet and add the red sauce. Cook until thicker, stirring occasionally. Mix in chili and pimento strips.
5. To serve, put the codfish on a platter, pour the sauce over it, and garnish with whole olives and parsley. Accompany with cooked rice.

About 4 servings

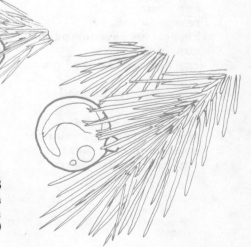

Baked Eel

Have eel skinned, split and backbone removed. Cut into 2 or 3 inch pieces, wash in salted water and dry thoroughly. Dredge with flour, season with salt and pepper, place in buttered baking pan and add ½ cup water. Cover. Bake in hot oven (400°F.) for 20 minutes or until eel is browned.

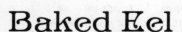

Pickled Octopus

1	small octopus (about 2 pounds)
½	cup olive oil
¼	cup white wine vinegar
	Juice of ½ lemon
1	tablespoon minced parsley
½	teaspoon marjoram
	Salt and pepper to taste

1. Beat octopus with the flat side of a metal meat hammer 15 to 20 minutes; it will feel soft and excrete grayish liquid.
2. Wash octopus thoroughly, drain, and cook in skillet without water until it becomes bright pink. Cut into bite-size pieces.
3. Make a salad dressing of the olive oil, vinegar, lemon juice, parsley, marjoram, salt, and pepper. Mix well.
4. Pour over octopus and store in the refrigerator in a covered container for 5 days before serving.
5. Serve cold as an appetizer.

4 to 6 servings

Oysters Piquante In The Half Shell

1	qt. (about 36) large oysters
1	cup mayonnaise
2	tablespoons chili sauce
1	tablespoon butter or margarine, melted
1½	teaspoons prepared mustard
1	teaspoon lemon juice
4	drops Tabasco
¼	teaspoon salt
	Few grains pepper
1/8	teaspoon paprika
1	cup buttered soft bread crumbs

1. Set out 12 small shell-shaped ramekins. (If oysters are purchased in shells, use deep half of each shell.)
2. Drain oysters; discard liquor; place 3 oysters in each ramekin or shell.
3. Blend the mayonnaise, chili sauce, butter, mustard, lemon juice, Tabasco, and a mixture of salt, pepper, and paprika. Spoon mayonnaise mixture over oysters. Top with the buttered crumbs.
4. Broil about 3 inches from source of heat 5 minutes, or until oysters begin to curl at edges and crumbs are golden brown.

12 servings

Crab Ravigote

¼	cup butter
¼	cup flour
1	teaspoon salt
	Few grains cayenne pepper
2	cups milk
⅔	cup chopped cooked green pepper
⅔	cup coarsely chopped pimento
2	tablespoons capers
2	teaspoons tarragon vinegar
2	cups lump crab meat
⅔	cup Hollandaise Sauce

1. Heat butter in cooking pan of a chafing dish; blend in flour, salt, and cayenne pepper; heat until bubbly. Gradually add milk, stirring constantly. Cook and stir until boiling; cook 1 minute.
2. Stir in remaining ingredients and heat thoroughly over simmering water.
3. Serve on **rusks.**

4 servings

Hollandaise Sauce: In the top of a double boiler, beat **2 egg yolks, 2 tablespoons cream, ¼ teaspoon salt** and a **few grains cayenne pepper** until thick with a whisk beater. Set over hot (not boiling) water. Add **2 tablespoons lemon juice or tarragon vinegar** gradually, while beating constantly. Cook, beating constantly with the whisk beater, until sauce is consistency of thick cream. Remove double boiler from heat, leaving top in place. Beating constantly, add ½ **cup butter,** ½ teaspoon at a time, until the butter is melted and thoroughly blended in.

About 1 cup

Fried Shrimp De Luxe

2 lbs. Cooked Shrimp
2 eggs, fork beaten
1½ cups of corn flake crumbs
1 env. (about 1⅜ oz.) dry onion soup mix
¼ cup chopped parsley
3 tablespoons shredded Parmesan cheese
Butter or margarine

1. Dip shrimp into egg, then into a mixture of the corn flake crumbs, soup mix, parsley, and cheese. (Store leftover crumb mixture, tightly covered, in refrigerator to use for coating meat, poultry, and shellfish, or as topping for casseroles.)
2. Fry the shrimp until lightly browned in hot butter in a heavy skillet.
3. Serve immediately.

About 8 servings

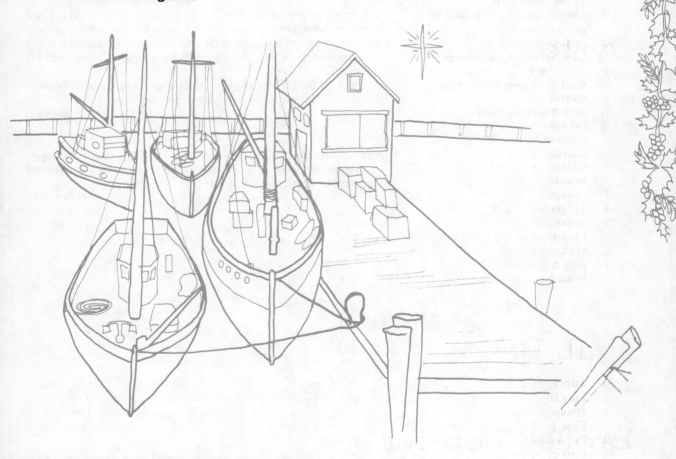

Broiled Scallops

1 pound scallops
French Dressing (page 46)
(Seasoned crumbs)

1. Dip scallops into French dressing and roll in crumbs.
2. Place on greased baking sheet in a preheated broiler (550°F.) and cook for about 15 minutes, or until the scallops are browned.
3. Turn occasionally.

Serves 4

Use a fork when dipping scallops into crumbs to make crust smooth and even.

Stuffed Squid

32	squid, cleaned and tentacles removed
¾	cup olive oil
1	large onion chopped
1½	cups water
1	cup long-grain rice
½	cup chopped parsley
1	teaspoon mint
1	teaspoon basil
2	cloves garlic, crushed in a garlic press
½	cup pine nuts
¼	cup dried black currants
1	cup dry white wine
	Salt and pepper to taste
	Water
	Juice of 2 lemons

1. Reserve squid. Rinse tentacles in cold water. Drain and mince finely.
2. In a large saucepan, heat 2 tablespoons of the oil, add onion and minced tentacles and cook over low heat until tentacles turn pink. Add water. Heat to boiling. Reduce heat, add rice, parsley, mint, basil, garlic, pine nuts, currants, and ½ cup of the wine.
3. Simmer until liquid is absorbed. Season with salt and pepper. Cool.
4. Using a teaspoon, stuff each squid cavity loosely with the rice mixture. Arrange squid in rows in a large baking dish. Combine the remaining wine and olive oil with enough water to reach half the depth of the squid. Season with additional salt and pepper. Cover.
5. Bake at 325°F about 40 minutes, or until squid is tender. Drizzle with lemon juice just before serving.

8 servings

Note: Stuffing may also be used as a side dish. Stuff 16 squid. Put remaining stuffing in a baking dish. Add a little water, salt and pepper and cover. Bake at 325°F 30 minutes.

Broiled Lobster

Kill lobster by inserting sharp knife into joint where tail and body-shell come together, thus cutting the spinal cord. Place lobster on back, make deep incision at mouth and with a quick cut, split lobster legthwise to end of tail. Open and remove stomach, intestinal vein running length of body, liver and coral. Save liver and coral for sauce. Crack large claws. Spread lobster as flat as possible, place split side up on greased broiler; brush with melted butter, sprinkle lightly with salt and pepper. Broil slowly for 15 to 20 minutes or until delicately browned. Turn and broil 10 minutes longer on shell side. Serve at once with melted butter. Allow ¾ to 1 pound lobster per portion.

Baked Lobster — Prepare lobster as above, but bake in hot oven (425°F.) 15 to 20 minutes, instead of broiling.

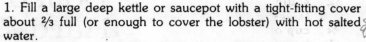

"Boiled" Lobster

Hot salted water (1 tablespoon salt per qt. water)
1   live lobster, about 1½ lbs
Fresh dill or parsley
Sauce for Lobster

1. Fill a large deep kettle or saucepot with a tight-fitting cover about ⅔ full (or enough to cover the lobster) with hot salted water.
2. Bring water rapidly to boiling. Grasp lobster by the back and plunge head first into the water.
3. Cover, bring water again to rolling boil. Reduce heat and simmer 15 to 20 min. Drain and cover with cold water to chill. Drain again. Place shell-side down on a cutting board.
4. Twist off the two large claws, the smaller ones and the tail. With a pair of scissors cut or with a sharp knife slit the bony membrane on the underside of tail. Remove and discard the intestinal vein. Using a sharp knife, cut completely through tail crosswise into 1½ in. pieces. With a sharp knife, cut lobster into halves; cut completely through entire length of body and through shell. Remove and discard the intestinal vein running lengthwise through center of body. Remove and discard stomach (a small sac which lies in the head) and spongy lungs (which lie in upper body cavity between meat and shell).
5. If present, remove and reserve the tomalley (green liver) and the coral (bright red roe) to be used along with the lobster meat or as a garnish. Using a sharp knife, cut the body crosswise into 1½-in. pieces.
6. Chill pieces of lobster and the claws in refrigerator. When ready to serve on the smorgasbord, arrange pieces of lobster and claws on a platter, shell-side up, to resemble a whole lobster. Garnish lobster with fresh dill or parsley.
7. Serve with Sauce for Lobster.

About 8 to 10 servings

Note: To use cooked lobster meat in food preparation, do not cut lobster into pieces. Spread tail shell apart and remove meat in one piece; remove meat from body shell. Disjoint the large claws and crack with a nutcracker. A nut pick may be helpful in removing meat from small joints and claws. Chill in refrigerator, cut and use as directed.

1¼ cups lobster meat

Lobster Fra Diavolo

Marinara Sauce (page 48)
2   live lobsters (about 1½ pounds each)
½   cup red wine
Few grains cayenne pepper

1. Prepare Marinara Sauce.
2. While sauce is cooking, fill a large, deep kettle about two thirds full with water. Bring to boiling and plunge lobsters, one at a time, head first into boiling water. Cover and boil about 8 minutes (Lobsters will turn pink.) Remove lobsters with tongs. With a sharp knife, slit underside lengthwise and remove stomach, lungs, and vein. Keep warm.
3. When sauce is cooked, stir in wine and cayenne, bring to boiling, and pour over lobsters. Serve immediately.

2 servings

Boiled Hard-Shelled Crabs

Drop live crabs one at a time into boiling salted water to cover. Reheat water to boiling after adding each crab. Cook 20 to 25 minutes, drain and rinse.

Break off claws. Remove the hard top shell, working from tail end. Discard the spongy fiber and apron. Crack claws with a nut cracker. Remove meat, discarding all body spines. A 1-pound crab will yield about 1 cup of meat. Crab meat may be used instead of lobster in most recipes for lobster meat.

Clams

There are two general types of clams, the soft clams and the hard or quahog clams. The latter group is divided into 3 classes: The littlenecks, small in size; the cherry stone, medium-sized; and the large chowder clams. The littleneck and cherry stone clams may be used uncooked.

When purchased the shells should be tightly closed or close at a touch as an indication of freshness. They may be opened with a knife or steamed open.

Steamed Clams

Wash clams in several waters, scrubbing shells well to remove any sand. Place in large kettle, using ½ cup of water to cover bottom of kettle. Cover kettle tightly, place over low heat and steam until shells open (about 15 minutes). Serve in the shells in soup plates, accompanying each serving with a small dish of melted butter to which a few drops of lemon juice have been added, and a cup of the hot clam liquor.

Steamed Mussels: Wash and cook mussels as above. Trim and discard horny beard. Serve as directed for Steamed Clams.

Clams for cocktails should be very chilly morsels; the sauce hot and spicy.

Vegetables

Cooked Artichokes

4 artichokes
1 tablespoon lemon juice
1 teaspoon salt
  Lemon slices
  Parsley sprigs
  Hot melted butter or margarine

1. Set out a large saucepot or kettle.
2. With a sharp knife cutting straight across, cut off 1 in. of the tops from artichokes.
3. Cut off stems about 1 in. from base and remove outside lower leaves. With scissors, clip off tips of uncut leaves and discard. Rinse artichokes under cold water and stand them upright in the saucepot. Add boiling water to a depth of 1 in. and lemon juice and salt.
4. Cook, covered, 35 to 45 min., or until a leaf can be easily pulled from artichoke. (Cooking time will depend upon size of artichokes.) If more water is needed during cooking, add boiling water.
5. Remove artichokes and drain upside down so all the water can run out. Cut off remainder of artichoke stem.
6. Serve immediately standing upright on serving platter. Garnish with lemon slices and parsley sprigs.
7. Accompany with individual serving of hot melted butter or margarine or individual servings of Hollandaise Sauce (page 18).

How to Eat Artichokes: Pull off each leaf and dip in melted butter or sauce. Eat only the tender part of leaf by drawing it between teeth. Discard less tender tip. Continue with each leaf until choke or fuzzy part in center is reached. Remove choke with knife and fork and discard. The heart or base may be eaten by cutting it with a fork and dipping each piece into the melted butter sauce.

4 servings

Chilled Artichokes: Follow recipe for Cooked Artichokes. Drain artichokes and chill in refrigerator until ready to serve. Chilled artichokes are usually served as a salad on individual serving plates. Accompany with individual servings of **mayonnaise, French Dressing** or any of its variations.

Carrot Ring

2 cups diced Cooked Carrots
½ teaspoon minced onion
1 teaspoon salt
⅛ teaspoon pepper
3 eggs, well beaten
1 cup milk

1. Combine ingredients. Pour into a buttered ring mold and bake in a moderate oven (350°F.) 40 minutes. Unmold and fill with seasoned Cooked Peas.

Serves 6

Helpful Hints About Vegetables

• To freshen fresh asparagus, stand the stalks upright in icy cold water.
• To remove the skins from carrots easily, cover them with boiling water and let stand for a few minutes until the skin loosens.
• To keep cauliflower white while cooking, use half milk and half water; cook, uncovered, until just tender.
• To make celery curls, cut stalks (about 3 inches long) lengthwise into thin strips to within 1 inch of end. Place in cold water until strips begin to curl.
• To make celery very crisp, let stand in icy cold water to which 1 teaspoon sugar per quart of water has been added.
• To garnish lettuce leaves sprinkle some paprika on waxed paper and dip edges of leaves into it.
• To keep onions from affecting eyes, peel them under running water.
• To prevent odor while cooking onions and cabbage, add 1 tablespoon lemon juice or a wedge of lemon to the cooking water.
• To extract juice from onion, cut a slice from the root end and scrape juice from center outward, using edge of a teaspoon.
• To finely cut onion, peel, cut off a slice, then cut exposed surface into 1/8-inch squares as deep as is needed. Then slice across thinly.
• To keep fresh parsley, mint, and watercress fresh and crisp, wash thoroughly, shake off excess water, and place uncrowded in a glass jar; cover and refrigerate.
• To freshen withered parsnips, carrots, potatoes, cabbage, lettuce, etc., let stand in icy cold salted water.
• To keep leftover pimientos from spoiling, put into a small jar, pour enough cooking or salad oil over top to cover, and place, tightly covered, in refrigerator.
• To keep potato skins soft and tender enough to eat, grease them before baking.
• To prevent sweet potatoes and apples from discoloring after paring, place them in salted water at once.
• To remove skin from a tomato quickly, place fork through stem end and plunge tomato into boiling water for a few seconds, then into cold water. Or hold tomato over direct heat for a few seconds; remove from heat and break the skin at blossom end; peel skin back.

Mushrooms with Sour Cream

1	large onion, minced
2	tablespoons butter
1	pound fresh mushrooms, diced
1	tablespoon flour
½	teaspoon salt
¼	teaspoon pepper
½	cup whipping cream
½	cup dairy sour cream
¼	cup grated cheese (Parmesan, Swiss, or Cheddar)
2	tablespoons butter, melted

1. Saute onion in 2 tablespoons butter in a skillet 5 minutes. Add mushrooms; saute 5 minutes longer.
2. Blend flour, salt and pepper with skillet mixture. Add whipping cream and sour cream gradually; mixing thoroughly. Turn into 1-quart casserole. Top with cheese. Drizzle melted butter over top.
3. Bake at 350°F about 20 minutes, or until thoroughly heated.

4 to 6 servings

Fried Mushrooms

½	lb. mushrooms
¼	cup butter or margarine
1	teaspoon minced parsley

1. Clean and slice mushrooms.
2. Heat in skillet butter or margarine.
3. Add mushrooms to skillet. Cook slowly, occasionally moving and turning gently with a spoon, until mushrooms are tender and lightly browned. Sprinkle with parsley.
4. Put mushrooms into a warm dish and serve immediately.

2 servings

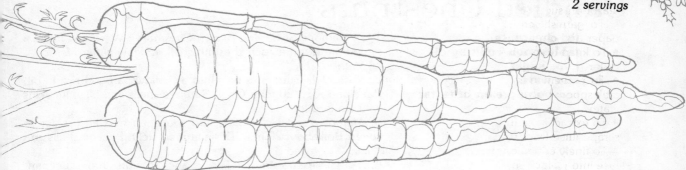

Mushrooms Magnifique

12	large fresh mushrooms, cleaned
2	tablespoons butter or margarine, softened
½	clove garlic, minced
¼	teaspoon salt
⅛	teaspoon thyme
½	cup finely chopped pecans
1½	tablespoons chopped parsley
½	cup heavy cream

1. Remove stem from mushrooms; finely chop enough stems to make ¼ cup; salt caps lightly.
2. Mix butter with garlic, salt, thyme, pecans, parsley, and chopped mushroom stems until well blended.
3. Heap mixture into mushroom caps and place in a shallow baking dish. Pour cream over all.
4. Heat in a 350°F oven 20 minutes, or until mushrooms are tender, basting several times.

12 Stuffed Mushrooms

Herbed Stuffed Mushrooms

¾ **pound mushrooms, chopped**
¼ **teaspoon salt**
⅛ **teaspoon freshly ground pepper**
1½ **teaspoons snipped fresh or ½ teaspoon dried basil leaves**
1 **tablespoon snipped parsley**
½ **cup chopped onion**
8 **large mushrooms, stems removed and sliced into rounds; reserve caps**
2 **tablespoons brandy**
1 **tablespoon clarified butter Parsley for garnish (optional)**

1. Process ¾ pound mushrooms, the salt, pepper, basil, parsley, and onion in a food processor or blender until thick and smooth. Layer ½ cup of the mushroom mixture in bottom of a baking dish.
2. Mix sliced mushroom stems, brandy, and butter. Fill reserved mushroom caps with mixture; place filled caps in baking dish. Spoon remaining mushroom mixture around mushrooms.
3. Bake at 400°F 20 minutes. Garnish with parsley.

4 servings

Note: This recipe is also excellent for a first course.

*If desired, chop mushrooms in food processor or blender, following manufacturer's directions.

Candied Chestnuts

1 **lb. chestnuts**
1 **tablespoon cooking oil**
2 **cups sugar**
1 **cup water**
⅛ **teaspoon cream of tartar**

1. *To Remove Shells and Blanch Chestnuts*—Wash and make a slit in both sides of each chestnut shell. *(Follow either Method 1 or Method 2)*
2. *Method 1:* Turn chestnuts into a shallow pan and mix in oil. Bake at 450°F 20 min. Cool. Remove shells and all inner skins with a sharp knife.
3. *Method 2:* Put chestnuts into saucepan and add water to cover. Boil about 20 min. Drain immediately. Peel off shells and skins.
4. *To Glaze Chestnuts*—Turn blanched nuts into saucepan. Cover with boiling salted water. Cover. Simmer 8 to 20 min., or until tender when pierced with a fork. Set aside to drain.
5. Lightly butter a baking sheet.
6. Combine sugar, water and cream of tartar in the top of a double boiler with a tight-fitting cover. Stir over low heat until sugar is dissolved.
7. Increase heat to medium and bring mixture to boiling. Cover double boiler top and boil mixture gently 5 min. (This will dissolve any crystals that may have formed on sides of pan.) Uncover and continue cooking without stirring. Using a pastry brush dipped in water, wash down crystals from sides of pan from time to time during cooking. Cook to 300°F (remove from heat while testing). Immediately set double boiler top over gently boiling water.
8. If syrup becomes too thick, place over direct heat until proper consistency. With fork or candy dipper, dip nuts into syrup. Remove when they appear clear. Drain over saucepan for a moment. Dry on prepared baking sheet.

About 1 lb. Candied Chestnuts

Roast Chestnuts

4 pounds chestnuts

1. Cut a cross on the flat side of each chestnut with a small sharp knife, being careful not to damage nutmeat. Spread in a large baking pan.
2. Roast in a 425°F oven about 30 minutes, or until done; shake frequently. Serve hot.

Cooked Asparagus

2 pounds asparagus
Boiling water
1 teaspoon salt

1. Wash the asparagus throughly and tie in 1 bundle or into 6 to 8 individual bundles. Place bundles upright with stems down in just enough boiling water to cover thick part of stalks.
2. Add salt and cook 10 minutes or until stalks are tender. Arrange bundles in water so tips are covered and cook 5 minutes longer. To serve season with pepper and butter.

Serves 6 to 8

With Hollandaise — Serve hot cooked Asparagus with Hollandaise Sauce (page 18) poured across the bunches and strip of pimiento over the sauce.

With Cheese Sauce — To vary, serve with Cheese Sauce (page 48).

Broccoli with Buttery Lemon Crunch

½ cup coarse dry bread crumbs
¼ cup butter
1 tablespoon grated lemon peel
3 tablespoons butter
1 small clove garlic, minced
½ teaspoon salt
Few grains pepper
1½ pounds broccoli, cooked and drained

1. Lightly brown crumbs in ¼ cup butter in a large skillet. Remove from butter with slotted spoon and mix crumbs with lemon peel.
2. Put the 3 tablespoons butter, garlic, salt and pepper into cooking pan of a chafing dish. Heat until butter is lightly browned. Add broccoli and turn gently until well coated with butter. Top with "lemoned" crumbs.

About 6 servings

Brussels Sprouts and Grapes

1½ pounds fresh Brussels sprouts, cut in half
1½ cups beer
2 teaspoons clarified butter
¼ teaspoon salt
⅛ teaspoon freshly ground white pepper
1 cup seedless white grapes
Snipped parsley

1. Simmer Brussels sprouts in beer in covered saucepan until tender (about 8 minutes); drain.
2. Drizzle butter over sprouts; sprinkle with salt and pepper. Add grapes; heat thoroughly. Sprinkle with parsley.

4 to 6 servings

Baked Potatoes

This is one of the most desirable methods of preparation. When potatoes are scraped and baked or baked in the skins, they retain most of their vitamins and minerals. If a soft skin is desired rub with fat before baking. Always break the skin immediately upon removal from the oven so steam may escape or potatoes will be soggy. Baked stuffed Irish potatoes when combined with poached eggs, chipped beef or sausage form attractive entrees for luncheons. Potatoes baked in the pan with meat absorb the delicious flavor of the meat besides serving as a garnish for the meat platter. Potatoes may be combined with meat or other vegetables and baked en casserole for one dish meals.

Mashed Potatoes

There are endless ways in which mashed potatoes may be combined and served. Preparing light and fluffy mashed potatoes, however, is an art. Add hot milk to boiled potatoes and beat hard with a potato masher or a fork, being sure no lumps remain in the potatoes. A very small amount of baking powder may be added to keep the potatoes white and light, but only hard beating will make them creamy. Be sure they are very hot when served. One pound or 3 medium-sized potatoes will make 2 cups mashed potatoes.

Idaho Potatoes On The Half Shell

6   medium potatoes
2   teaspoons prepared mustard
1   tablespoon grated onion
    Worcestershire sauce
½   teaspoon salt
    Buttered crumbs

1. Scrub potatoes and parboil for 20 to 30 minutes or until nearly cooked through.
2. Split partially cooked potatoes lengthwise into halves.
3. Spread each half with mustard, onion, sprinkle with Worcestershire sauce and salt. Top with buttered bread crumbs and bake in very hot oven (450°F.) 15 to 20 minutes or until potato is completely cooked and crumbs are brown.

Serves 6

4. If desired, use 3 large potatoes allowing ½ potato for each serving. Instead of buttered crumbs, use chopped bacon.

Slit baked potatoes as soon as they come from the oven, season and serve piping hot.

Fluffy Whipped Potatoes

6	medium (about 2 lbs.) potatoes
4	tablespoons butter
½	cup hot milk or cream(adding gradually)
¾	teaspoon salt
¼	teaspoon paprika
¼	teaspoon pepper

1. Wash, pare and cook potatoes.
2. Cook about 25 to 35 min., or until potatoes are tender when pierced with a fork. Drain. Heat potato masher, food mill or ricer and a mixing bowl by scalding them with boiling water. Mash or rice potatoes thoroughly. Whip in butter, milk or cream and a mixture of salt, paprika and pepper until potatoes are fluffy.
3. Whip potatoes until light and fluffy. If necessary, keep potatoes hot over simmering water and cover with folded towel until ready to serve.

About 6 servings

Mashed Turnips: Follow recipe for Fluffy Whipped Potatoes. Substitute washed, pared and quartered **turnips** for the potatoes. Omit milk or cream and paprika.

Hashed Brown Potatoes: Follow recipe for Fluffy Whipped Potatoes. Do not mash or rice. Dice potatoes and mix with **1 teaspoon salt** and **¼ teaspoon pepper.** Heat **⅓ cup fat** in a skillet. Add the potatoes, pressing into an even layer. Cook over low heat until a brown crust is formed on the bottom. Loosen edges and bottom of potatoes; shake skillet back and forth occasionally to prevent burning while browning. When potatoes are done. Lightly fold in half and serve on a warm platter.

Fried Parsnip Cakes: Follow recipe for Fluffy Whipped Potatoes. Substitute washed, pared and quartered **parsnips** for the potatoes. Cook about 30 min., or until tender. Omit paprika and add **2 tablespoons all-purpose flour.** Shape parsnip mixture into flat cakes. Heat about **¼ cup fat** in a skillet. Cook parsnip cakes over medium heat until golden brown and crisp on one side. Turn cakes and brown second side. Add extra fat when necessary.

Whipped Potato Ring: Follow recipe for Fluffy Whipped Potatoes. Spoon whipped potatoes onto warm serving platter to form a ring. Draw tines of fork around ring for patterned effect.

Scalloped Potatoes

6	medium potatoes
	Salt and pepper
2	tablespoons flour
4	tablespoons butter
	Milk

1. Pare potatoes and cut into thin slices. Place in a greased baking dish in 3 layers 1 inch deep, sprinkling each layer with salt, pepper and flour and dotting with butter.
2. Add milk until it can be seen between slices of potato, cover and bake in moderate oven (350°F.) until potatoes are tender when pierced with a fork, 1 to 1¼ hours. Remove cover for the last 15 minutes to brown.
3. Serve from baking dish.

Serves 6

Sweet Potatoes With Orange

4 medium (about 1⅓ lbs.)
sweet potatoes
¼ cup sugar
4 teaspoons grated orange
peel
½ teaspoon salt
¼ teaspoon cinnamon
2 large oranges
¼ cup butter
½ cup orange juice

1. Grease a 1½-qt. casserole with a tight-fitting cover.
2. Scrub sweet potatoes.
3. Cook, covered, in boiling salted water for 10 min. Drain. Shake pan over low heat to dry potatoes. Peel. With a sharp knife, cut into crosswise slices ⅛ in. thick. Set aside.
4. Mix sugar, orange peel, salt and cinnamon. Wash oranges, cut away peel and cut into crosswise slices ¼ in. thick.
5. Set out butter.
6. Arrange one half of the potato slices in an even layer in the casserole. Cover with one half of the orange slices and sprinkle with one half of the sugar mixture. Dot with 2 tablespoons of the butter. Repeat layering. Pour orange juice over all.
7. Cover; cook in a 375°F oven about 40 min., or until potatoes are tender when pierced with a fork.

About 4 servings

Maple Candied Sweet Potatoes

6 medium sweet potatoes
½ cup maple syrup
1 tablespoon butter
1 teaspoon salt
1 cup apple cider
½ cup water

1. Boil potatoes in jackets until nearly tender.
2. Peel and slice into baking dish.
3. Heat remaining ingredients to boiling, pour over potatoes and bake in slow oven (300°F.) 1 hour.

Serves 6

Maple Sweet Potatoes And Apples

6 medium (about 2 lbs.)
sweet potatoes
1 cup maple syrup
Few grains salt
4 large apples (about 1½
lbs.)
⅓ cup buttered crumbs

1. Butter a 1½-qt. baking dish.
2. Wash, scrub and cook sweet potatoes.
3. Cook 30 to 35 min., or until tender when pierced with a fork.
4. Meanwhile, measure into a saucepan maple syrup.
5. Add salt.
6. Wash, quarter, core, peel and thinly slice apples.
7. Add apples to saucepan and cook over low heat until apples are just tender. Carefully turn apple slices to cook evenly. Remove from heat and set aside. Peel the cooked sweet potatoes. Cut into thin, crosswise slices. Arrange one half of the potato slices in the baking dish. Top with one half of the apple slices and syrup. Repeat layers, using remaining potatoes, apples and syrup. Sprinkle with buttered crumbs.
8. Bake at 350°F about 10 min., or until crumbs are lightly browned.

6 to 8 servings

Golden Glow Sweet Potatoes

6	medium (about 2 lbs.) sweet potatoes, cut into halves or quarters
12	marshmallows (3 oz.)
4	tablespoons butter or margarine
½	cup cream or milk
¼	cup firmly packed brown sugar
¾	teaspoon salt
1	teaspoon nutmeg
½	teaspoon cinnamon

1. Grease a 1½-qt. casserole.
2. Wash sweet potatoes and cook covered in boiling salted water to cover.
3. Cook about 20 min., or until tender when pierced with a fork. Drain. To dry potatoes, shake pan over low heat. Peel; mash or rice.
4. Meanwhile, cut marshmallows into crosswise halves and set aside.
5. Whip in butter or margarine and cream or milk until potatoes are fluffy and a mixture of brown sugar, salt, nutmeg and cinnamon.
6. Fold one half of the marshmallow slices into potatoes; pile lightly into casserole.
7. Bake at 350°F 15 min. Remove from oven and arrange remaining marshmallows around top of casserole. Bake 15 to 20 min. longer, or until marshmallows are lightly browned.

6 servings

Glazed Grapefruit Sweet Potatoes: Follow recipe for Golden Glow Sweet Potatoes. Omit marshmallows. Wash **1 grapefruit.** With a sharp knife, cut into ¼ in. crosswise slices; cut each into halves. Dip slices into mixture of **¼ cup honey** and **2 tablespoons melted butter or margarine.** Arrange a wheel of overlapping slices over potatoes in casserole. Drizzle remaining honey mixture over top. Bake 20 to 25 min., or until grapefruit is slightly browned.

Pecan Sweet Squash: Follow recipe for Golden Glow Sweet Potatoes. Use **3 pkgs. (10 oz. each) frozen squash;** cook following directions on package. If squash seems dry, moisten with necessary amount of **cream** or **orange juice.** Otherwise, omit cream and whip butter into squash. Turn squash into casserole; top with **½ cup (about 2 oz.) coarsely chopped pecans.** Bake 15 to 20 min., or until heated and nuts are toasted.

Glazed Sweet Potatoes

6	sweet potatoes
1	cup brown sugar
¼	cup water
	Salt and pepper
	Butter

1. Boil potatoes until tender, drain and skin. Make a thick syrup of sugar and water.
2. Cut each potato in half, dip it in the syrup and place in a baking dish; season each piece with salt, pepper and butter.
3. Bake in a moderate oven (375°F.) until the potatoes are brown, about 15 minutes, basting occasionally with the syrup.

Serves 6 to 8

4. Add ½ cup sliced Brazil nuts and 6 cloves to the syrup.

Stuffed — Hollow centers from halves before glazing. Fill glazed potatoes with mincemeat or Cranberry Sauce. Heat throughly in oven.

Sweet Potatoes in a Basket

4   **medium (about 1¾ lbs.)
sweet potatoes**
3   **large oranges**
2   **tablespoons brown sugar**
1   **teaspoon salt**
6   **marshmallow halves**

1. Scrub and rinse sweet potatoes.
2. Cook, covered, in boiling salted water 30 to 35 min., or until potatoes are tender when pierced with a fork.
3. While potatoes cook, cut oranges into halves crosswise.
4. With a spoon or grapefruit knife, remove pulp sections from inside dividing membranes. With scissors or knife trim and remove membranes from orange shells. Set aside orange shells, cut-sides down, to drain thoroughly.
5. Peel potatoes. Pour boiling water over potato masher, food mill or ricer and bowl to heat thoroughly. Mash or rice potatoes into bowl.
6. Add to potatoes the orange pulp and a mixture of brown sugar, and salt.
7. Whip until light and fluffy. Pile lightly into orange shells. Top each with one of marshmallow halves.
8. Place filled basket on broiler rack. Place in broiler with tops of marshmallows about 4 in. from heat until marshmallows are browned and slightly melted.

6 servings

Whipped Sweet Potatoes

6   **medium (about 2 lbs.)
sweet potatoes, cut in
quarters**
2   **tablespoons butter or
margarine**
½   **cup hot milk or cream
(adding gradually)**
½   **teaspoon salt**

1. Wash, scrub and cook sweet potatoes covered in boiling salted water to cover .
2. Cook about 20 min., or until potatoes are tender when pierced with a fork. Drain and peel sweet potatoes.
3. To dry potatoes, shake pan over low heat. To heat potato masher, food mill or ricer and a mixing bowl, scald them with boiling water.
4. Mash or rice potatoes thoroughly. Whip in butter or margarine, milk or cream and salt until potatoes are fluffy.
5. Whip potatoes until light and fluffy. If necessary, keep potatoes hot over simmering water and cover with folded towel until ready to serve.

About 3 cups whipped potatoes

Mellow Sweet Potato Bake: Follow recipe for Whipped Sweet Potatoes. Grease a 1½-qt. baking dish. Substitute **orange juice** for milk or cream. Blend into whipped potatoes a mixture of **½ cup (about 2 oz.) chopped pecans, ⅓ cup firmly packed brown sugar, 1 teaspoon cinnamon** and **½ teaspoon nutmeg.** Spoon into baking dish. Cut **6 marshmallows** into halves; arrange them on top of potatoes. Put baking dish under broiler with top of food 4 in. from heat. Broil until marshmallows are delicately browned and slightly melted.

Baked Turnips

2	pounds turnips
¼	cup butter
1½	teaspoons salt
1½	teaspoons sugar
⅓	cup water

1. Pare turnips and cut into cubes.
2. Place in baking dish with remaining ingredients.
3. Cover closely and bake in moderate oven (350°F.) about 1 hour or until tender.

Serves 6 to 8

Creamed Onions and String Beans

8	small Cooked Onions
3⅓	cups Cooked Green Beans
1	recipe White Sauce (page 47)
	Paprika

1. Combine vegetables and white sauce and heat thoroughly. Sprinkle with paprika.

Serves 6 to 8

Glazed Onions

8	small (about 1 lb.) onions
¼	cup butter
2	tablespoons brown sugar

1. Clean onions.
2. Cook 15 to 25 min., or until onions are just tender.
3. Meanwhile, melt butter in a skillet.
4. Add and stir in brown sugar.
5. Stir over low heat until sugar is dissolved. Drain onions thoroughly. Dry onions by shaking pan over low heat. Add to butter-sugar mixture in skillet. Simmer a few minutes, or until onions are glazed. Turn several times to glaze.

4 servings

Creamed Onions: Follow recipe for Glazed Onions. Omit brown sugar mixture. Prepare **1 cup Thin White Sauce** (page 47); add onions and heat thoroughly.

Peas And Onions With Lemon Butter

2	pkgs. (10 oz. each) frozen green peas
2	teaspoons sugar (added to cooking water)
1	jar (16 oz.) whole white onions
3	tablespoons butter or margarine
1	tablespoon brown sugar
½	teaspoon salt
¾	teaspoon pepper
1	tablespoon lemon juice
¼	cup water

1. Set out a heavy 1½-qt. saucepan.
2. Cook green peas and sugar until tender, following package directions, and drain thoroughly.
3. Meanwhile, drain onions.
4. Chop enough drained onions to yield ½ cup chopped. Set remaining onions aside.
5. Heat in saucepan butter or margarine.
6. Add chopped onion and cook over medium heat 5 min. Stir in brown sugar, salt, pepper, lemon juice and water.
7. Heat 2 to 3 min., then add cooked peas and remaining whole onions. Toss lightly and continue cooking until thoroughly heated.

About 8 servings

Roast Turkey 36
Spicy Cranberry Sauce 46

Meat & Poultry

Cooked Whole Country Ham

Country-style ham, 14 to 16 lbs.

1. Scrub country-style ham thoroughly with warm water, rinse and put into a large kettle with a tight-fitting cover. (If a large kettle is not available, whole ham may be cut into halves and each piece cooked separately until done.)

2. Cover ham completely with cold water, cover kettle and bring to boiling. Pour off water and again cover ham with cold water. Cover and bring to boiling. Reduce heat and simmer, covered, 4 to 6 hrs., or until internal temperature reaches 170°F. Internal temperature is obtained by inserting roast meat thermometer into center of thickest part of lean at this time, being sure bulb does not rest on bone or in fat.

3. Remove ham from kettle. Allow to stand 15 or 20 min. before slicing. This allows meat to set and become easier to slice. Serve ham either hot or cold, cut into thin slices.

4. If desired, cook only half of ham; store uncooked half in refrigerator for future use.

Baked Country Ham: Follow recipe for Cooked Whole Country Ham. Remove ham from kettle about ½ hr. before done. Remove rind (if any), being careful not to remove fat. Making diagonal cuts, score fat surface of ham to form a diamond pattern. Place **whole cloves** in centers of diamonds. Place ham, fat side up, on a rack in a shallow roasting pan. Spread glaze over ham and bake at 300°F 30 to 40 min., or until ham tests done with a meat thermometer and glaze is set.

For Glaze—Mix in a small bowl **1 cup firmly packed brown sugar, 1 tablespoon all-purpose flour** and **teaspoon dry mustard**. Blend in **2 tablespoons vinegar** until smooth. Spread on ham.

How to Carve

Whole Ham

1. Ham is placed on platter with decorated or fat side up and shank to carver's right. Location of bones in right and left hams may be confusing so double check location of knee cap which may be on near or far side of ham. Remove two or three lengthwise slices from thin side of ham which contains knee cap.

2. Make perpendicular slices down to leg bone.

3. Release slices by cutting along leg bone.

Poultry

Standard Style

1. To remove leg (drumstick and thigh), hold the drumstick firmly with fingers, pulling gently away from body of bird. At the same time cut through skin between leg and body.

2. Press leg away from body with flat side of knife. Then cut through joint joining leg to backbone and skin on the back. Hold leg on service plate with drumstick at a convenient angle to plate. Separate drumstick and thigh by cutting down through the joint to the plate.

3. Slice drumstick meat. Hold drumstick upright at a convenient angle to plate and cut down, turning drumstick to get uniform slices. Drumsticks and thighs from smaller birds are usually served whole.

4. Slice thigh meat. Hold thigh firmly on plate with a fork. Cut slices of meat parallel to the bone.

5. Cut into white meat parallel to wing. Make a cut deep into the breast to the body frame parallel to and close to the wing.

6. Slice white meat. Beginning at front, starting halfway up the breast, cut thin slices of white meat down to the cut made parallel to the wing. The slices will fall away from the bird as they are cut to this line. Continue carving until enough meat has been carved for first servings. Carve more as needed.

Side Style

1. Remove wing tip and first joint. Grasp wing tip firmly with fingers, lift up, and cut between first and second joint. Place wing tip and first joint portion on side of platter. Leave second joint attached to bird.

2. Remove the drumstick. Grasp end of drumstick and lift it up and away from the body, disjointing it from the thigh. Thigh is left attached to the bird. Place drumstick on service plate for slicing. Hold drumstick upright at an angle and cut down toward plate, parallel with bone, turning to make even slices.

3. Anchoring the fork where it is most convenient to steady the bird, cut slices of thigh meat parallel to the body until the bone is reached. Run the point of the knife around the thigh bone, lift up with fork, and remove bone. Slice the remaining thigh meat.

4. Begin at front end of bird and slice white meat until the wing socket is exposed. Remove second joint of wing. Continue slicing until enough slices have been provided, or until the breastbone is reached.

5. Remove stuffing from hole cut into cavity under thigh. Slit the thin tissue in the thigh region with tip of knife and make an opening large enough for a serving spoon. Stuffing in breast cavity may be served by laying the skin back.

Roast Turkey I

1. Rinse bird with cold water. Drain and pat dry with absorbent paper or soft cloth.
2. Prepare cooked giblets and broth for gravy (see instructions).
3. Prepare favorite stuffing.
4. Rub body and neck cavities with salt. Fill lightly with stuffing. (Extra stuffing may be put into a greased covered baking dish or wrapped in aluminum foil and baked with turkey the last hour of roasting time.)
5. Fasten neck skin to back with skewer and bring wing tips onto back. Push drumsticks under band of skin at tail, or tie with cord. Set, breast up, on rack in shallow roasting pan. Brush with melted fat.
6. If meat thermometer is used, place it in center of inside thigh muscle or thickest part of breast meat. Be sure that tip does not touch bone. If desired, cover top and sides of turkey with cheese-cloth moistened with melted fat. Keep cloth moist during roasting by brushing occasionally with fat from the bottom of pan.
7. Roast, uncovered, at 325°F until turkey tests done (the thickest part of the drumstick feel soft when pressed with fingers and meat thermometer registers 180°F to 185°F).
8. When turkey is two thirds done, cut band of skin or cord at drumsticks. Roast until done. For easier carving, let turkey stand 20 to 30 minutes, keeping it warm. Meanwhile, if desired, prepare gravy from drippings.
9. Remove cord and skewers from turkey and place on heated platter. Garnish platter and, if desired, put paper frills on drumsticks.

Note: If desired, turkey may be roasted in heavy-duty aluminum foil. Brush bird thoroughly with melted fat; wrap securely in foil; close with a drugstore or lock fold to prevent leakage of drippings. Place, breast up, in roasting pan (omit rack). Roast a 10-to 12-pound turkey at 450°F about 3 hours. About 20 minutes before end of roasting time, remove from oven. quickly unfold foil to edge of pan. Insert meat thermometer. Return uncovered bird to oven and complete cooking. (Turkey will brown sufficiently in this time.)

Cooked Giblets And Broth: Put turkey neck and giblets (except liver) into a saucepan with 1 large onion, sliced, parsley, celery with leaves, 1 medium-sized bay leaf, 2 teaspoons salt, and 1 quart water. Cover and simmer until giblets are tender, about 2 hours; add the liver the last 15 minutes of cooking. Strain; reserve broth for gravy. Chop the giblets; set aside for gravy.

For paper frills: Select a sheet of white paper twice as wide as desired for length of frills; fold lengthwise. With fold toward you, make parallet cuts through fold 1/8 inch apart to within 1/2 inch of opposite side. Cut paper desired length; turn inside out. Wind around drumsticks. Fluff fringed ends with fingers. Fasten in place with cellulose tape.

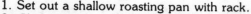

Roast Turkey II

1 turkey 10 to 12 lbs. ready-
  to-cook weight
  Herb Stuffing (page 44) or
  Oyster Stuffing (page 45)
2 teaspoons salt
  Melted Fat

1. Set out a shallow roasting pan with rack.
2. Clean and cut off neck of turkey at body (leaving on neck skin).
3. Prepare Herb Stuffing or Oyster Stuffing.
4. Rub neck and body cavities of turkey with salt .
5. Lightly fill body and neck cavities with stuffing. To close body cavity, sew or skewer and lace with cord. Fasten neck skin to back with skewer. Push drumsticks under band of skin at tail, if present, or tie them to tail. Bring wing tips onto back. Place breast-side up on rack on roasting pan. Brush thoroughly with melted fat.
6. If meat thermometer is used, place it in center of inside thigh muscle. (When done, meat thermometer will register (180°-185°F.)
7. Roast uncovered at 325°F 3½ to 4½ hrs. When two-thirds done, cut cord of band of skin at drumsticks. Continue roasting until thickest part of drumstick feels soft when pressed with fingers; protect fingers with cloth or paper napkin. If desired, baste or brush occasionally with butter or pan drippings.
8. Remove turkey from oven. Remove roast meat thermometer and keep turkey hot. Allow to stand about 20 min. before serving.
9. Remove cord and skewers. Serve turkey on a heated platter. Garnish with parsley and serve with Spicy Cranberry Sauce (page 46). If desired, put paper frills on drumsticks.

About 16 servings

Roast Chicken: Follow recipe for Roast Turkey. For turkey, substitute **1 roasting chicken,** 3 to 4 lbs., ready-to-cook weight. For rubbing cavities, reduce salt to ¼ to ½ teaspoon. Use one third recipe of stuffing. Chicken may be placed breast-side up or down. If placed down, turn breast side up when about three-quarters done. Roast at 375°F about 2¼ to 2¾ hrs.

Roast Goose With Baked Apples

8 pound goose
2 quarts bread crumbs
2 onions, chopped
2 tablespoons fat
1 teaspoon sage
2 teaspoons salt, Dash pepper
8 apples
¼ cup brown sugar
3 cooked mashed sweet-potatoes

1. Cook giblets (gizzard, heart and liver) until tender; chop and mix with bread crumbs, onion, fat, sage, salt and pepper.
2. Clean goose; remove fat from body cavity. Remove neck at body, leaving on neck skin. Rinse bird, pat dry. Rub cavities with salt. Spoon stuffing into body and neck; close cavity and fasten neck skin back with skewer.
3. Place, breast side down, on rack in roasting pan. Roast uncovered at 325°F. for 2½ hours. Drain off fat occasionally.
4. Turn goose, breast side up. Place apples in pan; bake 1 hour longer, or until goose tests done.
Baked Apples—Wash and core apples; sprinkle with brown sugar and stuff with seasoned sweet potatoes.

Serves 8

Roast Capon

6	pound capon
	Salt
4½	pounds sweet potatoes
¾	cup fat
2	cups marrons
	Chopped leaves 1 bunch celery
1	tablespoon minced onion
½	cup heavy cream

1. Dress capon, clean and rub inside well with salt. Boil enough sweet-potatoes to make 6 cups mashed.
2. Add salt and ½ cup fat. Mash marrons, reserving 6 for later use, and add to mashed potatoes; mix well.
3. Dice reserved marrons and stir into stuffing. Stuff capon with this mixture and close opening.
4. Rub the capon with unsalted fat.
5. Brown celery leaves and onion in remaining fat in roaster, breast up and cover with cloth.
6. Place capon on the sauteed leaves, dipped into melted fat. Bake in slow oven (325°F) 22 to 30 minutes per pound, basting frequently with melted fat. When capon is nearly tender, remove celery from pan. remove cloth and brush breast with the cream. Continue roasting until tender.
7. Prepare Gravy from the drippings in roaster, strain and serve with capon.

Serves 6 to 8

Roast Goose With Prune Stuffing

1	goose, 10 to 12 lbs. ready-to-cook weight
1	cup large dried prunes
2	cups water
1	tablespoon fat
1	lb. lean pork, coarsely ground
½	cup chopped onion
1	teaspoon salt
½	teaspoon pepper
1	egg yolk, slightly beaten
¼	cup chopped green olives
	Salt

1. Set out a shallow roasting pan with rack, a saucepan, and a skillet with cover.
2. Clean, cut off neck at body, leaving skin, and thoroughly wash in cold water, body and neck cavities of goose.
3. Drain and pat dry with absorbent paper. Set goose aside.
4. Put into the saucepan dried prunes and water.
5. Cover saucepan; bring to boiling and simmer prunes about 20 min., or until plump and tender. Slit prunes with a sharp knife and carefully remove pits. Set prunes aside.
6. Meanwhile, heat fat in the skillet.
7. Add lean pork and chopped onion.
8. Cook and stir over medium heat until meat is lightly browned. Season with salt and pepper.
9. Cover skillet and cook over low heat about 20 min.
10. Remove from heat and stir in egg yolk.
11. Remove ¼ cup of pork stuffing and combine with chopped green olives.
12. Fill prunes with this mixture and gently mix prunes with remaining stuffing.
13. Rub cavity of goose with salt.
14. Lightly fill body and neck cavities with stuffing. To close body cavity, sew or skewer and lace with cord. Fasten neck skin to back with skewer. Loop cord around legs and tighten slightly. Place breast-side down on rack in roasting pan.
15. Roast uncovered at 325°F for 3 hrs. Remove fat from pan several times during this period. Turn goose breast-side up. Roast 1 to 2 hrs. longer, or until it tests done. (Allow about 25 min. per pound for total roasting time.) To test for doneness, move leg gently by grasping end of drumstick; thigh joint should move easily.
16. Remove skewers and cord. Serve on heated platter. Garnish as desired.

8 servings

Goose Oriental

3 cups cooked goose meat, cut into 2-inch pieces
1½ cups canned pineapple juice
3 tablespoons lemon juice
¼ cup cornstarch
½ cup water
1 clove garlic, put through a garlic press
2 tablespoons cooking oil
1½ teaspoons salt
1 tablespoon brown sugar
½ teaspoon ginger
¼ teaspoon pepper
½ teaspoon allspice
½ teaspoon cinnamon
½ teaspoon cloves
½ teaspoon nutmeg
2 medium oranges, peeled and cut in segments

1. Place goose meat in a 1½-quart dish. Combine all remaining ingredients except orange segments and pour over goose. Cover and chill 2 to 3 hours.
2. Turn mixture into a large wok and cover. Bring to boiling and simmer 20 minutes, or until thoroughly heated. During last 5 minutes of cooking, place orange sections over goose; cover.
3. Serve with **hot fluffy rice** and pass bowls of **salted peanuts** and **fresh flaked coconut.**

6 servings

Glazed Duckling Gourmet

2 ready-to-cook ducklings, 4 lbs. each
½ teaspoons salt
¼ teaspoon nutmeg
4 tablespoons butter or margarine
1 clove garlic, minced
1½ teaspoons rosemary, crushed
1½ teaspoons thyme
1½ cups Burgundy
2 teaspoons red wine vinegar
⅓ cup currant jelly
2 tablespoons cold water
2 teaspoons cornstarch
1½ cups halved seedless green grapes

1. Rinse ducklings, pat dry and quarter.
2. Skin duckling pieces (do not use wings, necks and backs) and remove excess fat. Rub pieces with a mixture of salt and nutmeg.
3. Heat butter or margarine and garlic in a large skillet over medium heat.
4. Add duckling pieces and brown well on all sides. Sprinkle rosemary and thyme over duckling.
5. Add a blend of Burgundy, red wine vinegar and currant jelly.
6. Bring to boiling, cover skillet, lower heat and cook gently until duckling is tender, about 45 min. Remove duckling to a heated platter and keep warm.
7. Combine cold water and cornstarch, blending well.
8. Stir into liquid in skillet and bring to boiling. Cook and stir 1 to 2 min. Add seedless green grapes and mix lightly until thoroughly heated.
9. Pour the hot sauce over duckling; garnish platter with sprigs of **watercress.**

6 to 8 servings

Roast Duck

5   pound duck
    Salt, pepper, clove garlic
3   cups pared quartered ap-
    ples
1   cup seedless raisins
1   cup orange juice, if
    desired

1. Wash, singe and clean duck, season, rub with garlic and fill with apples mixed with raisins; place in pan and roast uncovered in slow oven (325°F.), allowing 20 to 30 minutes per pound.
2. Baste every 10 minutes using 1 cup of orange juice, if the flavor is desired.
3. Serve with Currant or Cranberry Jelly.

Serves 5

Pineapple Duck

1   duckling (about 3 pounds)
2   cups boiling water
    Salt and pepper
2   tablespoons soy sauce
1   can (20 ounces) pineapple
    chunks

1. Cut duckling into serving portions. Place in a large wok and cover with boiling water. Simmer, covered, until almost tender (about 1 hour).
2. Skim off fat. Stir in salt, pepper, soy sauce, and pineapple with syrup.
3. Cook 30 minutes, or until duckling is done.

4 servings

Rock Cornish Hens with Oranges and Almonds

1   Rock Cornish hen per ser-
    ving

For each serving:
2   tablespoons butter,
    melted
2   tablespoons orange juice
    Salt and pepper to taste
¼   teaspoon marjoram
¼   teaspoon thyme
½   garlic clove, crushed in a
    garlic press
½   navel orange with peel,
    cut in thin slices
2   tablespoons honey (about)
5   almonds, blanched,
    slivered, and toasted

1. Rinse hen well. Drain and pat dry. Place in a shallow baking dish. Drizzle inside and out with butter.
2. Combine orange juice, salt, pepper, marjoram, thyme, and garlic in a small bowl. Pour over and into the bird. Marinate 2 hours; turn occasionally.
3. Set bird on a broiler rack and put under broiler about 6 inches from heat. Broil 12 minutes on each side, or until tender, basting frequently with the marinade. During the last few minutes of broiling, arrange orange slices around the birds and drizzle with honey.
4. Garnish with almonds and serve at once.

Pasta & Rice

Lasagne Bolognese

3   tablespoons butter or
    margarine
3   tablespoons flour
1   cup milk
1   cup whipping cream
¼   teaspoon salt
    Dash of pepper
½   pound lasagne noodles
    Meat Sauce Bolognese
    (page 47)
1   cup (4 ounces) grated
    Parmesan cheese

1. Melt butter in saucepan; blend in flour. Gradually add milk and cream, stirring until thickened and smooth. Add salt and pepper.
2. Cook lasagne noodles in **boiling salted water** according to package directions. Drain, rinse, and spread on a damp towel.
3. Spread a thin layer of Meat Sauce Bolognese in a 13x9-inch baking dish. Top with a layer of half the lasagne noodles, half the Meat Sauce Bolognese, half the white sauce, and half the cheese; repeat layers.
4. Bake, uncovered, at 375°F 35 to 40 minutes, or until mixture is bubbly and top is golden brown. Let stand 10 minutes. Cut into squares to serve.

8 servings

Basic Noodle Dough

4   cups sifted all-purpose
    flour
½   teaspoon salt
4   eggs
6   tablespoons cold water

1. Sift flour and salt together into a large bowl.
2. Make a well in center of flour. Add eggs , one at a time, mixing slightly after each addition.
3. Add cold water gradually.
4. Mix well to make a stiff dough. Turn dough onto a lightly floured surface and knead. Proceed as directed in recipes.

Noodles with Poppy Seed and Raisins

2 cups cooked egg noodles
2 tablespoons butter, melted
1 can (12 ounces) poppy seed cake and pastry filling
1 teaspoon vanilla extract
1 teaspoon lemon juice
1½ teaspoons grated lemon peel
⅓ cup raisins

1. Toss noodles with butter in a saucepan.
2. Combine poppy seed filling with vanilla extract, lemon juice and peel, and raisins. Add to noodles and mix well. Cook just until heated through.

About 6 servings

Ravioli

Tomato Meat Sauce (page 47)
3 cups (about 1½ pounds) ricotta
1½ tablespoons chopped parsley
2 eggs, well beaten
1 tablespoon grated Parmesan cheese
¾ teaspoon salt
¼ teaspoon pepper
Basic Noodle Dough (page 41)
7 quarts water
2 tablespoons salt
Grated Parmesan or Romano cheese

1. Prepare Tomato Meat Sauce.
2. Mix ricotta, parsley, eggs, 1 tablespoon grated Parmesan, ¾ teaspoon salt, and pepper.
3. Prepare noodle dough. Divide dough in fourths. Lightly roll each fourth ⅛ inch thick to form a rectangle. Cut dough lengthwise with pastry cutter into strips 5 inches wide. Put 2 teaspoons filling 1½ inches from narrow end in center of each strip. Continuing along strip, put 2 teaspoons filling at 3½-inch intervals.
4. Fold each strip in half lengthwise, covering mounds of filling. To seal, press the edges together with the tines of a fork. Press gently between mounds to form rectangles about 3½ inches long. Cut apart with a pastry cutter and press cut edges of rectangles with tines of fork to seal.
5. Bring water to boiling in a large saucepot. Add 2 tablespoons salt. Add ravioli gradually; cook about half of ravioli at one time. Boil, uncovered, about 20 minutes, or until tender. Remove with slotted spoon and drain. Put on a warm platter and top with Tomato Meat Sauce. Sprinkle with grated cheese.

About 3 dozen ravioli

Perfection Boiled Rice

2 qts. water
1 tablespoon salt
1 cup uncooked rice

1. Bring water and salt to boiling in a deep saucepan.
2. Add uncooked rice gradually to water so boiling will not stop.
3. (The Rice Industry no longer considers it necessary to wash rice before cooking.) Boil rapidly, uncovered, 15 to 20 min., or until a kernel is entirely soft when pressed between thumb and finger.
4. Drain in colander or sieve and rinse with hot water to remove loose starch. Cover colander and rice with clean towel and set over hot water until kernels are dry and fluffy.

About 3½ cups cooked rice

Stuffing

Stuffing for a Small Turkey

½ cup butter
1 onion, minced
1 medium cooking apple, pared, cored, and diced
1 pound mushrooms, sliced
2 medium potatoes, boiled, peeled, and diced
½ cup pine nuts
½ cup dried black currants
1 cup blanched almonds, sliced
2 pounds chestnuts, boiled and cleaned
4 cups prepared bread stuffing
2 cups or more chicken stock to make a moist stuffing
1 can (4½ ounces) pate de foie gras
Salt and pepper to taste

1. Melt butter in a large deep skillet. Add onion, apple, and mushrooms; cook until tender.
2. Add potatoes, pine nuts, currants, almonds, chestnuts, stuffing, and stock. Heat thoroughly over low heat, adding more liquid if necessary.
3. Stir in pate. Season with salt and pepper.
4. Cool completely. Stuff bird.

Stuffing for a small turkey or 2 capons

Water Chestnut-Celery Stuffing

1 pkg. (8 oz.) stuffing mix
1 cup diced celery
¼ cup finely chopped onion
1 can (8 oz.) water chestnuts, drained and sliced
2 tablespoons dried parsley flakes

1. Prepare stuffing mix according to directions on package for moist stuffing.
2. Add celery, onion, water chestnuts, and parsley flakes; toss lightly to mix. Lightly spoon stuffing into body and neck cavities of bird (do not pack).

About 5⅓ cups stuffing

Apple Stuffing

2 medium-sized apples, pared and diced (about 2 cups, diced)
⅓ cup chopped celery with leaves
⅓ cup chopped onion
8 cups soft bread cubes
¾ cup melted butter
2 teaspoons salt
¼ teaspoon pepper
1 teaspoon marjoram
¾ cup apple cider

1. Combine apple, celery, and onion with bread cubes in a large bowl. Toss with butter, salt, pepper, and marjoram.
2. Pour cider over bread mixture and toss until thoroughly mixed. Spoon the stuffing lightly into neck and body cavities of bird (do not pack).

Stuffing for three 4-pound Ducklings

Herb Stuffing

¾ cup melted butter
2 teaspoons salt
1 teaspoon sage (or ½ teaspoon each of thyme, rosemary and marjoram)
¼ teaspoon pepper
2 qts. soft bread cubes
¾ cup milk
⅓ cup chopped celery with leaves
⅓ cup chopped onion

1. Mix butter, salt, sage and pepper.
2. In a large bowl, lightly toss mixture with bread cubes, milk, chopped celery with leaves, and chopped onion.
3. Spoon stuffing into neck and body cavities of turkey—do not pack. Stuff the turkey just before roasting. Extra stuffing may be place in greased, covered baking dish or wrapped in aluminum foil and baked with turkey the last hour of roasting time.

Stuffing for 10-lb. turkey

Note: Immediately after meal is served, remove stuffing from turkey. Store stuffing in a covered dish in refrigerator. If only one side of turkey has been carved, wrap remainder in waxed paper or aluminum foil. If more than one half of the meat has been carved off, remove remainder of meat from bone. Store covered in refrigerator.
This stuffing may also be used for chicken, goose or duckling. Allow about 1 cup bread cubes per pound of ready-to-cook weight of birds; if weight is 10-lbs. or less, subtract 1 cup from total; if weight is more than 10 lbs., subtract 2 cups from total. Proportionately decrease or increase the remaining ingredients in recipe. Mix diced apple with the stuffing before filling cavity of goose or duckling. Use ½ teaspoon marjoram instead of sage.

Walnut Poultry Stuffing

Giblets from 1 fowl
1   onion, sliced
1   bay leaf
1   cup boiling water
½   pound dry bread
1   tablespoon salt
2   tablespoons poultry
    seasoning or sage
2   cups chopped walnuts
4   tablespoons fat, melted

1. Cook giblets, onion and bay leaf in boiling water until tender.
2. Remove bay leaf, drain giblets and chop fine. Remove crusts from bread and break into fine crumbs.
3. Combine all ingredients and toss together lightly. Moisten with giblet stock. Will fill a 12 to 14 pound fowl.

Bread Stuffing

1½ pound loaf bread, dried
1   cup fat, melted
1   teaspoon salt
¼   teaspoon white pepper
¼   cup minced onion
2   tablespoons poultry
    seasoning

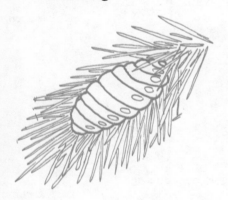

1. Remove crusts from bread and cut bread into 1-inch cubes. Toss all ingredients together lightly. Will fill a 6-pound fowl.
2. Stuffing does not necessarily need to be baked in the fowl or meat. If the bird is small or if there is some stuffing left over it may be baked or steamed in a greased ring mold, loaf or individual molds.
3. Fill center of ring with vegetables. Croquettes of stuffing may be served around bird.

Celery — Add 2 cups chopped celery, parboiled or uncooked.

Chestnut — Add 1 pound chestnuts, cooked and chopped.

Giblet — Add chopped, cooked giblets.

Mushroom — Add ¼ to ½ pound mushrooms, chopped and sauteed in 1 tablespoon butter for 5 minutes.

Olive — Add 1 cup or more coarsely chopped olives.

Oyster — Add 1 pint oysters, chopped, and heated in 2 tablespoons butter.

Irish Potato Stuffing

8   potatoes
4   tablespoons melted goose
    fat or butter
1   cup chopped onions
½   cup chopped celery
1   cup bread crumbs
½   teaspoon sage
1   teaspoon celery salt
½   teaspoon summer savory
1   teaspoon salt
¼   teaspoon pepper
2   eggs, beaten

1. Pare potatoes and cook until tender.
2. Drain and rice. Add remaining ingredients and mix well.
3. Will fill 10-pound goose.
4. Save potato water for basting goose during roasting.

Dressings & Sauces

Lime French Dressing

½ cup olive or salad oil
¼ cup lime juice
¼ cup lemon juice
½ teaspoon salt
   Few grains cayenne
2 tablespoons sugar or
   honey

1. Combine all ingredients.
2. Shake well before using.

Makes 1 cup

French Dresing

1 cup olive or salad oil
¼ cup vinegar
½ teaspoon salt
   Few grains cayenne
¼ teaspoon white pepper
2 tablespoons chopped
   parsley

1. Combine all ingredients.
2. Beat or shake thoroughly before using.

Makes 1¼ cups

Spicy Cranberry Sauce

2 cups (about ½ lb.)
   cranberries
1 cup sugar
1 cup water
1 piece (3 in.) stick cinnamon
⅛ teaspoon salt

1. Sort and wash cranberries.
2. Combine sugar, water, cinnamon stick, and salt in a 1-qt. saucepan and stir over low heat until sugar is dissolved.
3. Bring to boiling; boil uncovered for 5 min. Add the cranberries. Continue to boil uncovered without stirring, about 5 min., or until skins pop. Cool and remove cinnamon stick.
4. Serve with meat or poultry.

About 2 cups sauce

Medium White Sauce

2	tablespoons butter
2	tablespoons flour
1	cup milk
1/4	teaspoon salt
1/8	teaspoon pepper

Method 1—Melt butter and blend in flour. Add milk gradually, stirring constantly. Reduce heat and cook 3 minutes longer; add seasonings.

Method 2—Blend butter and flour together and add to hot milk, stirring constantly until mixture thickens. Cook 3 minutes longer; add seasonings.

Cream Sauce: Use cream for milk.

Thin White Sauce: Use 1 tablespoon butter and 1 tablespoon flour.

Tomato Sauce with Meat

1/4	cup plus 3 tablespoons olive oil
1/2	cup (about 1 medium) chopped onion
1/2	lb. beef chuck
1/2	lb. pork shoulder
1/2	lb. ground beef
7	cups canned tomatoes, sieved
1	tablespoon salt
1	bay leaf
3/4	cup (6-oz. can) tomato paste

1. Set out a large saucepot with a tight-fitting cover.
2. Heat 1/4 cup olive oil in sauceppot.
3. Add chopped onion and cook until lightly browned.
4. Add beef chuck and pork shoulder to skillet and cook, turning occasionally, until browned.
5. Add slowly a mixture of tomatoes, salt and bay leaf. Cover saucepot and simmer over very low heat, about 2 1/2 hrs.
6. Simmer uncovered over very low heat, stirring occasionally, about 2 hrs., or until thickened. If sauce becomes too thick, add 1/2 cup water.
7. Meanwhile, brown ground beef in 3 tablespoons olive oil, separating beef into small pieces with fork or spoon.
8. Remove beef chuck, pork shoulder and bay leaf from sauce.
9. Add ground beef to sauce and simmer 10 min. longer. Serve over cooked spaghetti.

About 4 cups sauce

Meat Sauce Bolognese

2	tablespoons butter
1	medium onion, finely chopped
1	small carrot, finely chopped
1	small stalk celery, finely chopped
3/4	pound ground beef
1/4	pound ground lean pork
1/4	cup tomato sauce or tomato paste
1/2	cup white wine
1	cup beef broth or stock
1/2	teaspoon salt
1/4	teaspoon pepper

1. Melt butter in a skillet. Stir in onion, carrot, and celery. Cook until tender. Add meat and cook over low heat 10 to 15 minutes.
2. Add tomato sauce, wine, 1/4 cup broth, salt, and pepper; mix well. Simmer about 1 1/4 hours. Stir in remaining broth, a small amount at a time, while the sauce is simmering. Sauce should be thick.

About 2 1/2 cups sauce

Cheese Sauce

2   tablespoons butter,
     melted
1   tablespoon flour
1   cup milk
     Dash salt and pepper
¾   cup American cheese,
     grated

1. Blend butter and flour together.
2. Add milk and boil until thickened.
3. Add seasonings and cheese and continue to heat, stirring constantly until cheese is melted.

Makes 1¾ cups

Marinara Sauce

2   medium cloves garlic,
      sliced
½   cup olive oil
1   can (28 ounces) tomatoes,
      sieved
1¼   teaspoons salt
⅛   teaspoon pepper
1   teaspoon oregano
¼   teaspoon chopped parsley

1. Brown garlic in hot olive oil in a large, deep skillet. Add gradually, stirring constantly, a mixture of the tomatoes, salt, pepper, oregano, and parsley. Cook rapidly uncovered about 15 minutes, or until sauce is thickened; stir occasionally. If sauce becomes too thick, stir in ¼ to ½ cup water.
2. Serve sauce hot on **cooked spaghetti.**

4 cups sauce

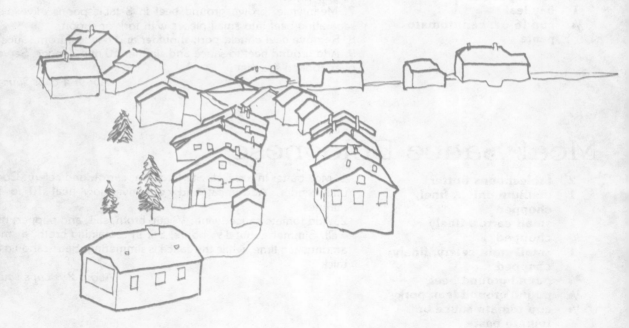

Cakes & Pies

Christmas Fruitcake

2	cups seeded raisins
4	cups seedless raisins
2	cups uncooked prunes
2	cups halved candied cherries
4	cups sliced citron
1	cup sliced candied pineapple
½	cup ground candied lemon peel
1	cup ground candied orange peel
3	cups broken walnut meats
1	tablespoon grated orange rind
½	cup fruit juice
5	cups sifted flour
1½	teaspoons salt
3	teaspoons baking powder
1	pound shortening
2	cups white sugar
1	cup brown sugar
3	teaspoons cinnamon
2	teaspoons cloves
1	teaspoon allspice
2	teaspoons mace
10	eggs, well beaten
1	tablespoon vanilla

1. Rinse raisins, drain, dry on a towel and slice seeded raisins.
2. Pour boiling water over prunes, cover and let stand 10 minutes; drain, dry and cut from pits into very small pieces.
3. Rinse, drain and dry cherries and citron before slicing.
4. Combine fruit, nuts and orange rind. Pour fruit juice over combined fruits.
5. Sift flour, salt and baking powder together.
6. Cream shortening, sugars and spices until fluffy. Add beaten eggs and mix thoroughly.
7. Add flour, prepared fruit mixture and flavoring and stir until fruits are well distributed. Pour into 1 10-inch tube pan and 1 loaf pan (about 10x5x3 inches) lined with 2 thicknesses of greased brown paper.
8. Smooth tops and decorate if desired.
9. Bake in very slow oven 275°F to 285°F.
10. Cake in tube pan will require from 3¾ to 4 hours baking time; in loaf pan, bout 3 to 3¼ hours.
11. Test with toothpick or cake tester before removing from oven. Baked weight approximately 10 pounds. May be served as soon as cool but improves if ripened a few days longer.

Helpful Hints About Cakes

‣ Use fluted paper baking cups when preparing cupcakes. They save greasing of pans and eliminate sticking. They also make pan washing easy.

• Line cake pans with baking parchment or waxed paper for easy removal of cakes after baking. Grease pans (bottoms only) before lining with paper and grease the paper. Cut several pieces at one time to fit pans and keep on hand for future use. (Cut the circles for layer cake pans about ¼ inch smaller than size of pan.) After baked cakes are removed from pans, peel off paper immediately.

• For baking fruitcake, line the pan with heavy brown paper extending 1 inch above top of pan. When cake is baked, place on wire rack. When completely cooled, lift cake from pan and peel off paper.

• When baking an upside-down cake, line cake pan with aluminum foil, folding foil over the edges of pan. After cake is baked, let cool on rack about 5 minutes. Then place serving plate on top of cake, turn cake upside down and remove the pan. Carefully lift off the foil. Cake comes out of pan easily and pan is easy to clean.

• When making cakes (or cookies) which use shortening and call for flavoring extracts and/or ground spices, add them to the shortening before creaming with the sugar. The fat "carries" the extract and spice flavors through the batter.

• To make a lace-like decoration on a sponge or angel food cake or other unfrosted cake, place a sheer, lace paper doily on top of cake; sift confectioners' sugar over top; then carefully lift off doily.

• To make your own cinnamon sugar to be used for sprinkling over warm, not-to-be-frosted cakes and cupcakes, combine *½ cup fine granulated sugar* with *1 tablespoon ground cinnamon*. Keep the mixture on hand stored in a covered jar.

• If cooked white frosting has "sugared" somewhat, beat in a small amount of *lemon juice* until frosting is smooth.

• To make marshmallow flowers for cake decorating, use large white or colored *marshmallows*. With kitchen shears dipped in water, cut off strips about 1/8 inch thick. Place strips between 2 pieces of waxed paper and roll with rolling pin to make thin "petals." Arrange petals on frosted cake to simulate flowers.

Currant Fruitcake

2	cups all-purpose flour
1	teaspoon baking powder
½	teaspoon salt
¼	teaspoon nutmeg
1	cup dried currants
¼	cup candied orange peel, chopped
¼	cup candied lemon peel, chopped
¼	cup candied cherries, halved
¼	cup candied apricots, chopped
¾	cup dark raisins
½	cup light raisins
¾	cup butter
⅔	cup sugar
3	eggs
½	cup blanched almonds, sliced

1. Preheat oven to 325°F. Grease a 9" tube pan.
2. Sift flour, baking powder, salt and nutmeg.
3. Mix currants, orange peel, lemon peel, apricots, cherries and raisins.
4. Beat butter and sugar until light and fluffy. Add eggs one at a time beating well after each addition.
5. Gradually add flour mixture and beat until well mixed.
6. Stir in fruit mixture until well mixed. Turn in prepared pan. Sprinkle with almonds. Gently press into top.
7. Bake 60-65 minutes till cake tester comes out clean. Cool on wire rack. Remove from pan after 15 minutes.

Regal Fruitcake

2	cups (about 8 oz.) walnuts
1	cup (about 7 oz.) date pieces
1	cup (about 8 oz.) maraschino cherries
1½	cups sifted all-purpose flour
1	teaspoon baking powder
½	teaspoon salt
3	eggs
¾	cup sugar
1	pkg. (6 oz.) semisweet chocolate pieces

1. Lightly grease bottom of 9x5x3-in. loaf pan. Line bottom and sides with parchment paper cut to fit pan. Lightly grease paper.
2. Coarsely chop walnuts and set aside.
3. Cut dates into small pieces and set aside.
4. Drain maraschino cherries, slice and set aside on absorbent paper. (A few pats with the paper will absorb the excess moisture from cherries.)
5. Sift all-purpose flour, baking powder and salt together and set aside.
6. Beat eggs until thick and piled softly.
7. Add sugar gradually, beating well after each addition.
8. Thoroughly blend in fruits, nuts and chocolate.
9. Mixing only until blended after each addition, add dry ingredients in thirds to egg-fruit mixture. Finally, mix only until blended. Turn batter into pan, spreading to edges.
10. Place a shallow pan containing 2 cups water on bottom rack of oven during baking period.
11. Bake at 300°F 1 hr. 45 min., or until cake test done.
12. Cool cake on cooling rack 10 min. before removing from pan. Run spatula gently around sides of pan. Cover with cooling rack. Invert. Turn right side up immediately after peeling off parchment paper.
13. Using a pastry brush, paint cake with brandy or apple cider. Cool thoroughly and wrap tightly in waxed paper, aluminum foil or moisture-vaporproof material. Store in cool place to age for 10 days before serving.

One 9x5-in. fruitcake

Chocolate Fruitcake

½ lb. (about 1¼ cups) diced assorted candied fruits
½ lb. candied red cherries, cut in quarters; about 1¼ cups, quartered
5 oz. (about 1 cup) golden raisins
⅓ cup water
⅓ cup rum
2¼ cups (about ¾ lb.) toasted salted almonds
4 oz. (4 sq.) unsweetened chocolate
2 cups sifted all-purpose flour
1 teaspoon baking powder
6 egg yolks
¾ cup butter
1½ cups sugar
6 egg whites

1. Two 1½-qt. molds will be needed.
2. Mix assorted candied fruits, cherries and raisins in a bowl.
3. Pour over the fruit a mixture of water and rum.
4. Cover tightly and allow to stand 8 hrs. or overnight.
5. Thoroughly grease molds and set aside.
6. Coarsely chop almonds and set aside.
7. Melt chocolate and set aside to cool.
8. Sift flour and baking powder together and set aside.
9. Beat egg yolks until thick and lemon-colored and set aside.
10. Cream butter until softened.
11. Add 1 cup sugar gradually, creaming until fluffy after each addition.
12. Add the beaten egg yolks in thirds, beating thoroughly after each addition.
13. Stir melted chocolate into creamed mixture. Alternately add dry ingredients in fourths and fruit mixture in thirds to creamed mixture. After each addition, beat only until batter is blended. Finally, beat only until batter is well blended (do not overbeat). Then mix in the chopped nuts.
14. Beat egg whites until frothy.
15. Add ½ cup sugar gradually.
16. Continue beating until rounded peaks are formed. Spread beaten egg whites over batter and gently fold together. Turn into prepared molds.
17. Bake at 250°F 2 hrs. to 2 hrs. 15 min., or until cake tests don. Cool completely on cooling rack before removing from pans. Wrap tightly in aluminum foil and store in cool place to age for several weeks before serving. Once or twice a week, using a pastry brush, paint cakes with rum and store again.

Two 2½-lb. Fruitcakes

Refrigerator Christmas Cake

2 tablespoons unflavored gelatin
1 quart milk
2 eggs, separated
¾ cup sugar
¼ teaspoon salt
¾ cup chopped maraschino cherries
⅓ cup maraschino juice
1 teaspoon vanilla
1½ cups heavy cream
2 dozen vanilla wafers

1. Soften gelatin in ½ cup milk.
2. Scald remaining milk and pour onto beaten egg yolks.
3. Add sugar, salt and softened gelatin; return to double boiler; cook until mixture coats a spoon. Cool.
4. Add cherries, juice and vanilla. Chill until mixture begins to thicken.
5. Fold in beaten egg whites and half the cream, whipped.
6. Butter a cake pan and arrange vanilla wafers around it.
7. Pour in fillng and cover top with remaining vanilla wafers.
8. Chill overnight.
9. Unmold and frost sides and top of cake with remaining cream, whipped.

Serves 12

Cream-Filled Chestnut Cake

1   **pound chestnuts in the shell; or use 1¼ cups pecans, chopped**
¾   **cup butter**
1   **cup sugar**
½   **teaspoon vanilla extract**
6   **eggs, separated**
1¼   **cups all-purpose flour**
1   **teaspoon baking powder**
½   **cup milk**
     Chestnut Cream

1. Prepare chestnuts (see Note).
2. Cream butter with sugar and vanilla extract until fluffy. Mixing well after each addition, add the chestnut puree, then the egg yolks, one at a time.
3. Mix flour with baking.powder, and add alternately with milk to the chestnut mixture, mixing well after each addition. Beat egg whites until stiff, but not dry. Fold into batter.
4. Turn mixture into 2 greased and floured 9-inch round layer cake pans.
5. Bake at 350°F about 25 minutes, or until done.
6. Let cool, then put layers together and decorate cake with chestnut cream.

One 9-Inch Layer Cake

Note: To prepare chestnuts, rinse chestnuts and make a slit on two sides of each shell. Put into a saucepan; cover with boiling water and boil about 20 minutes. Remove shells and skins; return chestnuts to saucepan and cover with boiling salted water. Cover and simmer until chestnuts are tender (10 to 20 minutes). Drain and finely chop.

Chestnut Cream: Prepare **¾ pound chestnuts** in the shell (see Note above); or use **1 cup pecans**, chopped. Whip **1 cup whipping cream** until thickened. Mix in **⅔ cup confectioners' sugar** and **½ teaspoon vanilla extract**, then chestnuts.

Pumpkin Cake

2¼   **cups sifted cake flour**
3   **teaspoons baking powder**
½   **teaspoon baking soda**
½   **teaspoon salt**
1½   **teaspoons ground cinnamon**
½   **teaspoon ground allspice**
½   **teaspoon ground ginger**
½   **cup butter or margarine**
½   **cup sugar**
1   **cup lightly packed dark brown sugar**
2   **eggs**
¾   **cup buttermilk**
¾   **cup canned pumpkin**
½   **cup finely snipped or chopped golden raisins**

1. Sift the flour, baking powder, baking soda, salt, and spices together and blend thoroughly; set aside.
2. Cream butter; gradually add sugars, creaming until fluffy. Add eggs, one at a time, beating thoroughly after each addition.
3. Beating only until smooth after each addition, alternately add dry ingredients in fourths and a mixture of the buttermilk, pumpkin, and raisins in thirds to creamed mixture. Turn batter into 2 prepared 9-inch layer cake pans and spread evenly.
4. Bake at 350°F about 30 minutes, or until cake tests done.
5. Cool and remove from pans as directed for butter-type cakes.

Two 9-Inch Cake Layers

Pumpkin Miniatures: Follow recipe for Pumpkin Cake. Spoon batter into 1¾-inch muffin-pan wells lined with paper baking cups, half filling each. Bake at 375°F about 13 minutes, or until cupcakes test done. Remove from pans and cool on racks. Frost with *butter cream frosting.*

6½ Dozen Cupcakes

Bohemian Christmas Twist

1	cake yeast
¼	cup lukewarm water
1	cup milk
½	cup sugar
¼	cup butter
2	eggs or 4 yolks
	Grated rind of 1 lemon
⅛	teaspoon mace
1	teaspoon salt
4¼	cups sifted flour
½	cup raisins
½	cup chopped blanched almonds
	Coffee Cake Icing (below)

1. Soften yeast in lukewarm water.
2. Scald milk and add sugar and butter. Cool to lukewarm.
3. Add softened yeast, beaten eggs, lemon rind, mace, salt and 2 cups flour. Beat well to make smooth batter. Cover and let rise until light.
3. Add raisins, nuts and remaining flour to make a dough just firm enough to be handled easily. Knead until smooth. Cover and let rise until doubled in bulk.
4. Punch down and divide dough into 3 large portions and 5 smaller ones.
5. Roll each portion into a long roll.
6. Braid the 3 larger rolls loosely and place on greased baking shett.
7. Then braid 3 of the smaller portions and place on top of the large braid.
8. Twist the last 2 portions together and place on top. Cover and let rise until light.
9. Brush with sweetened milk and bake in hot oven 400°F 45 minutes.
10. When cool, spread with icing and sprinkle with chopped nuts.

1 loaf

Coffee-Cake Icing

1	cup confectioners' sugar
2	tablespoons warm milk
½	teaspoon vanilla

Combine ingredients and mix thoroughly. Frosting for 1 (12-inch) coffee cake.

Christmas Wreath Ring

¼	cup softened butter
½	cup granulated sugar
2	tablespoons water
¼	cup candied cherries, halved
¼	cup citron, cut into strips
2	cups sifted flour
3	teaspoons baking powder
¾	teaspoon salt
4	tablespoons cold shortening
⅔	to ¾ cup milk
2	tablespoons melted butter
½	cup brown sugar
	Cinnamon
¼	cup currants

1. Spread softened butter in ring mold and pat granulated sugar over bottom and sides. Sprinkle water in mold.
2. Arrange cherries and citron in bottom to resemble holly.
3. Sift flour, baking powder and salt together. Cut in shortening.
4. Add milk to make a soft dough.
5. Turn out on lightly floured board and knead gently ½ minute.
6. Roll out in rectangle, 6 inches wide and ¼ inch thick.
7. Brush lightly with melted butter, and sprinkle with brown sugar, cinnamon and currants.
8. Roll like jelly roll and cut into 1½-inch slices. Place cut side down in mold.
9. Bake in hot oven 400°F 30 minutes.
10. Let stand in pan 1 minute after removing from oven.
11. Serve hot or cold.

1 9-inch ring or 12 rolls

Homemade Mincemeat

1 pound cooked lean roast beef, cut in pieces
½ pound suet
5 pounds tart apples
½ pound seedless raisins, chopped
1 pound dried currants
¼ pound candied citron, chopped
¼ pound candied orange peel, chopped
2 tablespoons grated orange peel
1 tablespoon grated lemon peel
¼ cup orange juice
2 tablespoon lemon juice
2 cups sugar
1 teaspoon cinnamon
½ teaspoon cloves
½ teaspoon nutmeg
½ teaspoon mace
½ teaspoon powdered coriander seed
1 teaspoon salt
½ teaspoon pepper
2 cups apple cider
1 can (16 ounces) tart red cherries (undrained)
½ pound walnuts, coarsely chopped
1 cup brandy

1. Finely chop meat and beef suet or put through coarse blade of food chopper, and put into a large electric cooker.
2. Wash, quarter, core, and pare the apples; coarsely chop or put through coarse blade of a food chopper (there should be about 6 cups chopped).
3. Add apples and all other ingredients, except nuts and brandy to cooker; stir.
4. Cover and cook on High 4 to 6 hours, stirring occasionally.
5. Stir in nuts.
6. Cover and cook on High 15 to 30 minutes.
7. Stir in brandy. Quickly ladle the mincemeat into hot, sterilized jars; seal.

About 7 (1-pint) jars

Cranberry Pie

4 cups cranberries
1½ cups sugar
2 tablespoons flour
¼ teaspoon salt
3 tablespoons water
1 tablespoon melted butter
1 recipe Plain Pastry (page 57)

1. Wash berries, chop and mix with sugar, flour, salt, water, and melted butter.
2. Line piepan with pastry, pour in filling and arrange strips of pastry over top in lattice design.
3. Bake in very hot oven 450°F 15 minutes; reduce to moderate 350°F and bake about 30 minutes longer.

1 9-inch pie

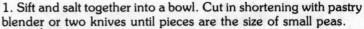

Pastry For 1-Crust Pie

1   **cup sifted all-purpose flour**
½   **teaspoon salt**
⅓   **cup lard, vegetable shortening, or all-purpose shortening**
3   **tablespoons cold water**

1. Sift and salt together into a bowl. Cut in shortening with pastry blender or two knives until pieces are the size of small peas.
2. Sprinkle the water over mixture, a teaspoonful at a time, mixing lightly with a fork after each addition. Add only enough water to hold pastry together. Work quickly; do not overhandle. Shape into a ball and flatten on a lightly floured surface.
3. Roll from center to edge into a round about ⅛ inch thick and about 1 inch larger than overall size of pan.
4. Loosen pastry from surface with spatula and fold in quarters. Gently lay pastry in pan and unfold it, fitting it to pan so it is not stretched.
5. Trim edge with scissors or sharp knife so pastry extends about ½ inch beyond of pie pan. Fold extra pastry under at edge, and flute.
6. Thoroughly prick bottom and sides of shell with a fork. (Omit pricking if filling is to be baked in shell.)
7. Bake at 450°F 10 to 15 minutes, or until crust is light golden brown.
8. Cool on rack.

One 8 or 9-inch Pie Shell

Pastry For 2-Crust Pie: Double recipe for Pastry For 1-Crust Pie. Divide pastry into halves and shape into a ball. Roll each ball as above. For top crust, roll out one ball of pastry and cut 1 inch larger than pie pan. Slit pastry with knife in several places to allow steam to escape during baking. Gently fold in half and set aside while rolling bottom crust. Roll second ball of pastry and gently fit pastry into pie pan; avoid stretching. Trim pastry with scissors or sharp knife around edge of pan. Do not prick. Fill as directed in specific recipe. Moisten edge with water for a tight seal. Carefully arrange top crust over filling. Gently press edges to seal. Fold extra top pastry under bottom pastry. Flute.

Pastry For Little Pies And Tarts: Follow recipe for Pastry for 1-Crust Pie. Roll pastry ⅛ inch thick and cut about ½ inch larger than overall size of pans. Carefully fit rounds into pans without stretching. Fold excess pastry under at edge. Flute. Prick bottom and sides of shell with fork. (Omit pricking if filling is to be baked in shell.) Bake at 450°F 8 to 10 minutes, or until light golden brown. Cool on wire rack.

Three 6-inch pies, six 3½ inch tarts, or nine 1½-inch tarts

Pecan Pie

¼   **cup butter**
⅔   **cup brown sugar, firmly packed**
¼   **teaspoon salt**
¾   **cup dark corn syrup**
3   **eggs, beaten**
1   **teaspoon vanilla**
½   **recipe Plain Pastry (page 57)**
1   **cup pecan halves**

1. Cream butter and sugar together until fluffy.
2. Add salt, corn syrup, eggs, and vanilla.
3. Line piepan with pastry and sprinkle with pecans; pour the filling over pecans.
4. Bake in very hot oven 450°F 10 minutes, reduce temperature to moderate 350°F and bake 35 minutes longer or until knife inserted in center comes out clean.

1 8-inch pie

Plain Pastry

2 cups sifted flour
¾ teaspoon salt
⅔ cup shortening
4 to 6 tablespoons cold water

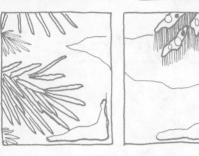

1. Sift flour and salt together and cut in shortening with 2 knives or pastry blender.
2. Add water, using only a small portion at a time, until mixture will hold together.
3. Divide dough into 2 parts.
4. Roll out on floured board to desired size.
5. Line the piepan with one piece of dough, being careful not to stretch dough.
6. After filling is placed in pastry; dampen edges of lower crust with cold water and cover with remaining dough which has been rolled out and slashed in several places to allow steam to escape while baking.
7. Press edges together with prongs of fork and bake according to recipe for filling selected.

2 9-inch shells for one 2-crust 9-inch pie

Christmas Tree: Mark to suggest branches and decorate with green sugar.

Santa Claus: Mark to suggest features and decorate with red sugar.

Mincemeat Pie

3½ cups Mincemeat (page 55; if using packaged condensed mincemeat, prepare according to package directions)
1 teaspoon grated lemon peel
1 tablespoon lemon juice
Pastry for 2-Crust Pie (page 56; use a 9-in. pie pan)

1. Mix Mincemeat, lemon peel and lemon juice in a saucepan.
2. Heat mixture thoroughly. Set aside to cool slightly.
3. Meanwhile prepare Pastry for 2-Crust Pie.
4. Fill pastry shell with mincemeat mixture. Complete as in Pastry for 2-Crust Pie.
5. Bake at 450°F 10 min. Reduce heat and bake at 350°F 40 min. longer, or until crust is light golden brown.
6. Cool on cooling rack.

One 9-in. pie

Mince Pie

Pastry for a 2-crust pie (page 56)
3½ cups moist mincemeat
1¼ cups chopped apple
1 teaspoon grated lemon peel
1 tablespoon lemon juice

1. Prepare a 9-inch pie shell; roll out remaining pastry for top crust. Set aside.
2. Blend mincemeat and remaining ingredients in a saucepan; heat thoroughly. Cool slightly.
3. Turn filling into unbaked pie shell. Complete as directed for 2-crust pie.
4. Bake at 425°F 35 minutes. Cool on wire rack.

One 9-Inch Pie

Cookies

Anise Cookies

1	package active dry yeast
½	cup warm water
2	teaspoons salt
5	cups all-purpose flour
3	tablespoons sugar
1	cup each butter and vegetable shortening (at room temperature)
4	teaspoons anise extract
1	teaspoon baking powder Red and green decorating sugar

1. Dissolve yeast in water in a large bowl. Add salt and about 1 cup flour; mix very well. Add all other ingredients except the remaining flour and baking powder; mix thoroughly. Add remaining flour and baking powder; mix well.

2. Make 6 or 8 balls; with the palm of your hand, make long, thin rolls (about the size of the ring finger) and cut them into squares.

3. Place pieces, leaving space between them, on a cookie sheet. Make a cut on top of each.

4. Bake at 350°F about 25 minutes, or until golden brown.

5. Remove from cookie sheets and coat with red and green sugar. Cool on wire racks.

About 10 dozen

Swedish Gingersnaps

1½	cups sifted all-purpose flour
1	teaspoon baking soda
1½	teaspoons ground ginger
1	teaspoon ground cinnamon
¼	teaspoon ground cloves
½	cup butter
¾	cup sugar
1	egg
1½	teaspoons dark corn syrup Whole blanched almonds, cut in small pieces

1. Sift flour, baking soda, and spices together; set aside.

2. Cream butter; add sugar gradually, beating until fluffy. Add egg and corn syrup and beat thoroughly.

3. Blend in dry ingredients in fourths, mixing thoroughly after each addition. Refrigerate dough several hours.

4. Using a portion of the dough at a time, roll about ¹⁄₁₆ inch thick on a lightly floured surface. Cut with lightly floured cookie cutters into various shapes. Transfer to ungreased cookie sheets. Place one almond piece in the center of each.

5. Bake at 375°F 6 to 8 minutes.

About 7 dozen cookies

Norwegian Christmas Cookies

1¾ cups sifted all-purpose flour
½ cup cornstarch
2 teaspoons baking powder
½ teaspoon salt
¼ to ½ teaspoon pepper
½ teaspoon ground cardamom
½ teaspoon ground cinnamon
½ teaspoon ground cloves
1 cup butter or margarine
¼ teaspoon vanilla extract
1 cup sugar
¼ cup cream
⅔ cup finely chopped blanched almonds

1. Sift flour, cornstarch, baking powder, salt, and spices together; set aside.
2. Cream butter with extract. Add sugar gradually, beating until light and fluffy.
3. Add dry ingredients alternately with cream, mixing after each addition. Stir in almonds.
4. Shape dough into ¾-inch balls; place 1 inch apart on ungreased cookie sheets.
5. Bake at 350°F about 15 minutes.

About 6 dozen cookies

Fig Cookies

2¼ cups sifted cake flour
½ teaspoon cinnamon
1 teaspoon soda
½ cup shortening
1 cup brown sugar
2 eggs, beaten
2 tablespoons sour cream
1 cup chopped figs

1. Sift flour, cinnamon and soda together.
2. Cream shortening with sugar until fluffy; add eggs, cream and figs.
3. Add sifted dry ingredients with more flour if necessary. Chill thoroughly.
4. Roll out on lightly floured board to ⅛-inch thickness, cut with cookie cutter and bake on greased cookie sheet in moderate oven 350°F 10 to 12 minutes or until browned.

5 dozen cookies

Christmas Cut Outs

½ cup shortening
1 cup sugar
1 egg
2 teaspoons baking powder
2½ cups cake flour
½ teaspoon salt
½ cup milk
1 teaspoon vanilla

1. Cream shortening well.
2. Add sugar and egg and blend together.
3. Sift baking powder, flour and salt together and add to creamed mixture alternately with the milk.
4. Stir in vanilla. Chill.
5. Roll out 1/16 inch thick on pastry cloth, cut in Christmas designs, brush with egg white, decorate and bake at 350°F 10 to 12 minutes.

100 2-inch cookies

Decoration—Cut cookies in the shape of Santa Claus, frost with red Confectioners' Icing. Using pastry tube, trim with white frosting making a white beard, fur collar and cuffs on pants, hat and jacket. Use raisins for eyes, nose and mouth.

Decorated Sugar Cookies

2½ cups sifted all-purpose
flour
¼ teaspoon baking powder
¼ teaspoon salt
1 cup butter or margarine
1¼ teaspoons vanilla extract
1 cup confectioners' sugar
1 egg yolk
2 teaspoons cream
Sugar, colored sugar,
chocolate sprinkles or
finely chopped nuts

1. Set out cookie sheets and cookie cutters.
2. Sift flour, baking powder and salt together and set aside.
3. Cream butter or margarine and vanilla extract until butter is softened. Add confectioners' sugar gradually, creaming until fluffy after each addition.
4. Mixing until well blended after each addition, add dry ingredients in fourths to creamed mixture.
5. Put one third of the dough on a lightly floured surface. Roll about ¼ in. thick. Cut out cookies with lightly floured cookie cutters. Transfer cookies to cookie sheets. Repeat for remaining dough. Set aside.
6. Beat egg yolk and cream together until blended. Brush over cookies. Sprinkle with sugar, colored sugar, chocolate sprinkles or finely chopped nuts.
7. Bake at 350°F 12 to 15 min. With spatula remove cookies to cooling racks.

4 to 5 doz. cookies

Belgian Christmas Cookies

⅔ cup butter
1 teaspoon almond extract
1 cup firmly packed dark
brown sugar
2 eggs
1⅔ cups sifted all-purpose
flour
1½ teaspoons baking powder
½ teaspoon salt
½ cup finely chopped
unblanched almonds
½ teaspoon ground cin-
namon
2 teaspoons red sugar
2 teaspoons green sugar

1. Cream butter with extract; add brown sugar gradually, creaming until fluffy. Add eggs, one at a time, beating thoroughly after each addition.
2. Sift flour, baking powder, and salt together; add in thirds to creamed mixture, mixing until blended after each addition. Turn into a greased 15x10x1-inch jelly roll pan and spread evenly to edges.
3. Sprinkle a mixture of almonds and cinnamon over batter, then sprinkle with a mixture of red and green sugars.
4. Bake at 375°F 10 to 12 minutes.
5. Cut into bars while still warm.

About 5 dozen cookies

Italian Butter Cookies

4 cups sifted all-purpose
flour
1 cup sugar
2½ teaspoons grated lemon
peel
1 tablespoon rum
4 egg yolks, beaten
1 cup firm unsalted butter,
cut in pieces
1 egg white, slightly beaten

1. Combine flour, sugar, and lemon peel in a large bowl; mix thoroughly. Add rum and then egg yolks in fourths, mixing thoroughly after each addition.
2. Cut butter into flour mixture with pastry blender until particles are fine. Work with fingertips until a dough is formed.
3. Roll one half of dough at a time about ¼ inch thick on a lightly floured surface. Cut into desired shapes. Brush tops with egg white. Transfer to lightly greased cookie sheets.
4. Bake at 350°F. about 15 minutes.

About 6 dozen cookies

Brown Moravian Cookies

4	cups sifted all-purpose flour
1/4	teaspoon baking soda
1/4	teaspoon salt
1	teaspoon ground cinnamon
1/2	teaspoon ground cloves
1/4	teaspoon ground ginger
1	cup firmly packed light brown sugar
1/2	cup butter
1/2	cup lard*
1 1/2	cups light molasses
1/2	teaspoon cider vinegar

1. Sift flour, baking soda, salt, and spices together into a large bowl. Add brown sugar; mix well.
2. Cut in butter and lard. Add molasses and vinegar gradually, mixing well. Chill dough thoroughly.
3. Using a small amount of dough at a time, roll out about 1/8-inch thick on a lightly floured surface. Cut with fancy cookie cutters. Transfer to greased cookie sheets.
4. Bake at 350°F 8 to 10 minutes.

About 6 dozen cookies

Note: *Use butter, if desired, but then cookie will not be authentic.

Lemon Snaps

1/3	cup shortening
1	cup sugar
5	egg yolks or 2 whole eggs
3	tablespoons milk
1 1/2	teaspoons lemon extract
3 2/3	cups cake flour
2 1/2	teaspoons baking powder
1/4	teaspoon soda
1/2	teaspoon salt
	Egg for glaze, Milk

1. Cream shortening and sugar.
2. Beat eggs well and add with the milk and lemon extract.
3. Mix and sift dry ingredients and add. Chill.
4. Roll 1/8 inch thick. Cut and brush tops with egg diluted with milk.
5. Bake in moderate oven (375°F) 10 minutes.

150 cookies 2 1/2-inch diameter

Note: If desired top each cookie with 1/2 almond before brushing with diluted egg. Decorate with narrow strips of candied ginger, pine apple, citron or lemon peel.

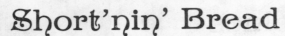

Short'nin' Bread

1   cup firmly packed light
brown sugar
4   cups sifted all-purpose
flour
1   lb. softened butter

1. Set out cookie sheets.
2. Press brown sugar through a sieve. Mix thoroughly with all-purpose flour.
3. Add butter and work in until a smooth dough is formed.
4. Turn onto a lightly floured surface and pat to ½-in. thickness. (If necessary, chill dough for easier handling.) Cut into desired shapes and transfer to cookie sheets.
5. Bake at 325°F about 25 min., until very delicately browned.
6. Remove sheets to cooling racks 5 min. before transferring cookies to racks to cool thoroughly.

3 to 4 doz. cookies

English Toffee Bars

1   cup butter
1   cup sugar
1   egg yolk
2   cups sifted all-purpose
flour
1   teaspoon ground cin-
namon
1   egg white, slightly beaten
1   cup chopped pecans
2   oz. (2 sq.) semisweet
chocolate, melted

1. Cream butter; add sugar gradually, beating until fluffy. Beat in egg yolk.
2. Sift the flour and cinnamon together; gradually add to creamed mixture, beating until blended.
3. Turn into a greased 15x10x1-inch jelly roll pan and press evenly. Brush top with egg white. Sprinkle with pecans and press lightly into dough.
4. Bake at 275°F 1 hour.
5. While still hot, cut into 1½-inch squares. Drizzle with melted chocolate. Cool on wire rack.

5 to 6 Dozen Cookies

Moji Pearls

¾   cup butter
½   teaspoon vanilla extract
⅓   cup sugar
1½   cups sifted all-purpose
flour
⅛   teaspoon salt

1. Cream butter with extract; add sugar gradually, beating until fluffy.
2. Blend flour and salt; add in thirds to creamed mixture, mixing until blended after each addition. Chill dough until easy to handle.
3. Shape into 1-inch balls or into crescents (if desired, roll in sesame seed). Place about 2 inches apart on ungreased cookie sheets.
4. Bake at 325°F 20 minutes.

About 3 Dozen Cookies

Pecan Poofs: Follow recipe for Moji Pearls. Substitute ¼ *cup confectioners' sugar* for sugar. Decrease flour to 1 cup. Mix in *1 cup pecans,* finely chopped. Shape dough into balls or pyramids.

Snowball Meltaways

1   cup butter
½   cup confectioners' sugar
1   teaspoon vanilla extract
2½   cups sifted all-purpose
     flour
½   cup finely chopped pecans

1. In a heavy saucepan over low heat, melt and heat butter until light brown in color. Pour into a small mixing bowl; chill until firm.
2. Cream browned butter with confectioners' sugar and extract until light and fluffy. Gradually add flour, mixing until blended. Stir in the pecans. Chill several hours for ease in handling.
3. Shape into 1-inch balls. Place on ungreased cookie sheets.
4. Bake at 350°F about 20 minutes.
5. Remove to wire racks. While still hot, dust with *confectioners' sugar.*

About 4 dozen cookies

Cherry Jewels

½   cup butter
1   teaspoon vanilla extract
¼   cup sugar
1   egg
1   teaspoon grated lemon
     peel
1   tablespoon lemon juice
1¼   cups sifted all-purpose
     flour
¾   cup finely chopped pecans
18   candied cherries, halved

1. Cream butter with extract and sugar until light and fluffy. Add the egg and lemon peel and juice; beat thoroughly. Gradually add flour, mixing until blended. Chill.
2. Shape dough into 1-inch balls, roll in chopped pecans and place on greased cookie sheets. Press a cherry half onto center of each ball.
3. Bake at 350°F 10 to 12 minutes.
4. Cool on wire racks.

3 dozen cookies

Honey Clusters

2 cups sifted all-purpose flour
¼ teaspoon salt
3 eggs
½ teaspoon vanilla extract
1 cup honey
1 tablespoon sugar
1 tablespoon tiny multicolored candies

1. Set out deep saucepan or automatic deep fryer for deep-frying and heat fat to 365°F.
2. Meanwhile, place flour and salt in a large bowl.
3. Make a well in center of flour. Add eggs, one at a time, mixing slightly after each addition.
4. Add vanilla extract. Mix well to make a soft dough.
5. Turn dough onto a lightly floured surface and knead. Divide dough into halves. Lightly roll each half ¼ in. thick to form a rectangle. Cut dough with a pastry cutter into strips ¼ in. wide. Use palm of hand to roll strips to pencil thickness. Cut into pieces about ¼ to ½ in. long.
6. Fry only as many pieces of dough as will float uncrowded, one layer deep in the fat. Fry 3 to 5 min., or until lightly browned, turning occasionally during frying time. Drain over fat before removing to absorbent paper.
7. Meanwhile, cook honey and sugar in skillet over low heat about 5 min.
8. Remove from heat and add deep-fried pieces. Stir constantly until all pieces are coated with honey-sugar mixture. Remove Strufoli with a slotted spoon and set in refrigerator to chill slightly. Remove to a large serving platter and arrange in a cone-shape mound.
9. Sprinkle with multicolored candies.
10. Chill in refrigerator. Serve by breaking off individual pieces.

8 to 10 servings

Pepparkakor

1 cup butter
1½ cups sugar
1 egg
1 tablespoon dark corn syrup
2¾ cups all-purpose flour
2 teaspoons baking soda
1 tablespoon cinnamon
2 teaspoons ginger
1 teaspoon ground cloves
Blanched almonds
Icing

1. Beat butter in a bowl until softened. Add sugar gradually, creaming well. Add egg and beat thoroughly. Blend in corn syrup.
2. Blend flour, baking soda, and spices; add to creamed mixture gradually, mixing until blended.
3. Chill dough until easy to handle.
4. Using a portion of the chilled dough at a time, roll dough on a lightly floured surface to ⅛-inch thickness. Cut with floured cookie cutters.
5. Transfer cookies to cookie sheets and decorate some with almonds.
6. Bake at 400°F 5 to 7 minutes. Remove immediately to wire racks.
7. Decorate cooled cookies with icing.

About 6 dozen cookies

Icing: Put **1 egg white** and ⅛ **teaspoon almond extract** into a small bowl. Add **2 cups sifted confectioners' sugar** gradually to egg white while mixing; beat until smooth and glossy.

Cinnamon Stars

⅓ cup plus 1 tablespoon egg whites
1 cup confectioners' sugar
1 teaspoon grated lemon peel
¾ teaspoon ground cinnamon
2 cups unblanched almonds, grated

1. Lightly grease 2 cookie sheets, sprinkle with **flour,** and shake off excess; set aside.
2. Using an electric beater, beat egg whites until stiff, not dry, peaks are formed. Add confectioners' sugar gradually, beating 5 minutes at medium speed. Remove ⅓ cup of meringue and set aside.
3. Into remaining meringue, beat the lemon peel and cinnamon. Fold in the almonds.
4. Turn almond mixture onto a pastry canvas sprinkled with **confectioners'** or **granulated sugar.** Gently roll ¼ to ⅜ inch thick. Lightly sprinkle with sugar. Cut with a 2-inch star-shaped cookie cutter dipped in confectioners' sugar.
5. Transfer to cookie sheets; drop about ½ teaspoonful of reserved meringue onto each star and spread out evenly onto points. Set aside in a warm place (about 80°F) 1½ hours.
6. Bake at 375°F 5 minutes.

About 3 dozen cookies

Kolacky Cookies

1 cup butter
8 oz. cream cheese, softened
¼ teaspoon vanilla extract
2¼ cups sifted all-purpose flour
½ teaspoon salt
Cherry preserves, apricot preserves, or prune filling

1. Cream butter and cream cheese with extract until fluffy.
2. Blend flour and salt; add in fourths to creamed mixture, mixing until blended after each addition. Chill dough thoroughly.
3. Roll dough ¼ inch thick on a floured surface; cut with 2-inch round cutter or fancy-shaped cutters. Transfer to ungreased cookie sheets, make a small indentation in center of each round, and fill with ½ teaspoon preserves.
4. Bake at 350°F 10 to 15 minutes, or until delicately browned.

About 3½ dozen cookies

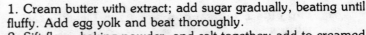

Spritz

1	cup butter
1	teaspoon vanilla extract
½	cup sugar
1	egg yolk
2	cups sifted all-purpose flour
½	teaspoon baking powder
¼	teaspoon salt

1. Cream butter with extract; add sugar gradually, beating until fluffy. Add egg yolk and beat thoroughly.
2. Sift flour, baking powder, and salt together; add to creamed mixture in fourths, mixing until blended after each addition.
3. Following manufacturer's directions, fill a cookie press with dough and form cookies of varied shapes directly onto ungreased cookie sheets.
4. Bake at 350°F 12 minutes.

About 5 dozen cookies

Chocolate Spritz: Follow recipe for Spritz. Thoroughly blend **¼ cup boiling water** and **6 tablespoons cocoa;** cool. Mix in after addition of egg yolk.

Nut Spritz: Follow recipe for Spritz. Stir in **½ cup finely chopped nuts** (black walnuts or toasted blanched almonds) after the last addition of dry ingredients.

Chocolate-Tipped Spritz: Follow recipe for Spritz. Dip ends of cooled cookies into Chocolate Glaze (below). If desired, dip into finely chopped **nuts,** crushed **peppermint stick candy,** or **chocolate shot.** Place on wire racks until glaze is set.

Marbled Spritz: Follow recipe for Spritz. Thoroughly blend **2 tablespoons boiling water** and **3 tablespoons cocoa;** cool. After the addition of egg yolk, remove a half of the creamed mixture to another bowl and mix in a half of the dry ingredients. Into remaining half of creamed mixture, stir cocoa mixture; blend in remaining dry ingredients. Shape each half of dough into a roll and cut lengthwise into halves. Press cut surfaces of vanilla and chocolate flavored doughs together before filling cookie press.

Spritz Sandwiches: Spread **chocolate frosting** or **jam** on bottom of some cookies. Cover with unfrosted cookies of same shape to form sandwiches.

Jelly-Filled Spritz: Make slight impression at center of cookie rounds and fill with **¼ teaspoon jelly** or **jam** before baking.

Chocolate Glaze: Partially melt **3 oz. (½ cup) semisweet chocolate pieces** in the top of a double boiler over hot (not simmering) water. Remove from heat and stir until chocolate is melted. Blend in **3 tablespoons butter.**

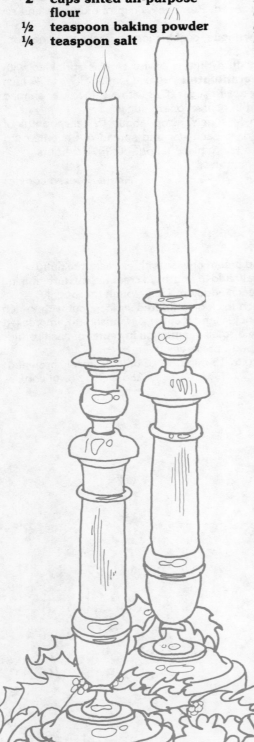

Weiser Lebkuchen

5	eggs, beaten
2	cups sugar
1	cup finely shredded citron
1/4	cup finely chopped candied cherries
3/4	cup almonds, finely chopped
4 1/2	cups cake flour
1/2	teaspoon cinnamon
1/2	teaspoon cloves
1/2	teaspoon nutmeg
1/2	teaspoon salt

1. Beat eggs till thick.
2. Add sugar gradually and beat well.
3. Add citron, cherries, almonds and the flour which has been sifted with the spices and the salt.
4. Roll and cut in squares.
5. Let stand overnight and bake in a moderate oven 350°F 15 to 20 minutes until a very light brown.

96 squares

Christmas Trees: Omit citron, cherries and almonds and proceed as in Weiser Lebkuchen recipe. Cut trees with a knife and cut away the edges of the tree with a corrugated cutter. Sprinkle liberally with green sugar. Ornament with colored candies and bake.

Christmas Wreaths: Omit citron, cherries and almonds and proceed as in Weiser Lebkuchen recipe. Cut with doughnut cutter. Sprinkle liberally with green sugar. Dot with tiny red candies and bake.

Spicy Ginger Crunchies

2 1/4	cups sifted all-purpose flour
2	teaspoons baking soda
1	teaspoon salt
1	teaspoon ground cinnamon
3/4	teaspoon ground ginger
1/2	teaspoon ground cloves
3/4	cup butter
1	teaspoon vanilla extract
1	cup sugar
1	egg
1/4	cup molasses

1. Sift flour, baking soda, salt, and spices together; set aside.
2. Cream butter with extract; gradually add sugar, beating until light and fluffy. Add egg and molasses; beat thoroughly.
3. Gradually add dry ingredients to creamed mixture, mixing until blended. Chill several hours.
4. Shape dough into 3/4-inch balls, roll in *sugar* and place 2 inches apart on greased cookie sheets.
5. Bake at 375°F 7 to 8 minutes.
6. Immediately remove to wire racks to cool.

6 to 7 Dozen Cookies

Old-Fashioned Sugar Cookies

1	cup shortening
1	cup sugar
2	eggs, beaten
2	teaspoons vanilla
1	cup sour cream
5	cups cake flour
2	teaspoons baking powder
1 1/4	teaspoons salt
1	teaspoon soda

1. Cream shortening and sugar.
2. Add eggs and vanilla to sour cream.
3. Sift together the flour, baking powder, salt and soda and add alternately with the liquid to shortening and sugar mixture. Chill thoroughly.
4. Roll out on pastry cloth 1/4 inch thick. Cut with large cutter, sprinkle with sugar and press in lightly.
5. Bake in moderate oven 375°F 15 minutes.

100 2 1/2-inch cookies

Bread Crumb Cookies

2/3 cup shortening
1 cup brown sugar
2 eggs, well beaten
1/2 cup molasses
2 1/2 cups fine bread crumbs
1 cup cake flour
1/2 teaspoon soda
1/4 teaspoon cloves
1/2 teaspoon cinnamon
1 teaspoon baking powder
Flour, Milk

1. Cream shortening and sifted sugar thoroughly.
2. Add beaten eggs and molasses.
3. Sift together dry ingredients and add slowly to the liquid mixture. Mix thoroughly.
4. Add enough additional flour to make a stiff dough. Chill and roll thin.
5. Use a simple cookie cutter.
6. Glaze by brushing tops with milk.
7. Bake at 350°F 6 to 8 minutes.

156 cookies of 2-inch diameter

Queenies

1 cup shortening
3/4 cup confectioners' sugar
2 cups cake flour
1 cup chopped nuts
1/2 cup flour
2 tablespoons confectioners' sugar

1. Cream shortening and sugar thoroughly. Add flour and nuts. Blend together.
2. Roll 1/4 inch thick on a pastry cloth which has been dusted with a mixture of 1/2 cup flour and 2 tablespoons sugar.
3. Cut into small fancy shapes with cookie cutters.
4. Arrange on a greased cookie sheet and bake in a hot oven (400°F) 10 minutes.
5. Sprinkle top of cookies with confectioners' sugar as soon as they are removed from the oven.

100 cookies

Variation—Add 1/4 teaspoon cinnamon to dough, blend well. Roll, cut and decorate with tiny red cinnamon candies.

Cheese Cookies

3	ounces cream cheese
½	cup butter
½	cup sugar
1	egg yolk
½	teaspoon vanilla
1	cup sifted flour
¼	teaspoon salt
⅛	teaspoon nutmeg

1. Blend cheese and butter together, add sugar and egg yolk and cream together thoroughly.
2. Add vanilla.
3. Sift remaining ingredients together and add to cream mixture.
4. Chill until firm enough to roll.
5. Roll out on lightly floured board, cut with cookie cutter and place on greased baking sheet.
6. Bake in moderate oven 375°F about 10 minutes.

24 cookies

Pastel Cookies

1	cup shortening
1	cup sugar
2	egg yolks
3¼	cups cake flour
1	teaspoon baking powder
¼	teaspoon salt
6	tablespoons milk
	Food colorings

1. Cream shortening and sugar thoroughly.
2. Add egg yolks and beat well.
3. Sift all dry ingredients together and add alternately with milk to the creamed mixture.
4. This foundation makes the following:

Checkerboard: Use ½ of recipe and divide into 2 portions, one portion slightly larger than the other. To the smaller quantity add 1 square of melted chocolate. Divide the white dough into 5 balls of equal size and the chocolate dough into 4 balls of equal size. Shape each ball into a roll 8 inches long, then flatten sides to form rectangle ½ inch thick. Stack on waxed paper: a white roll, a dark roll and then a white roll. The stacked rolls will be 3 squares wide and 3 squares high and the colors will be alternated to make a checkerboard. When stacking the rolls moisten each side before placing the next roll in position. Wrap the resulting cube in waxed paper and chill for at least 3 hours. Slice ⅓ inch thick and arrange on a well greased cookie sheet. Bake at 375°F 9 minutes.

80 cookies

Pinwheels: Use ¼ of the recipe and divide this into 2 portions. Color as desired. Any 2 colors can be used; however it is preferable to have one dark and one light, such as the chocolate and white combination for checkerboards. Roll out the dark layer first making it almost ½ inch thick. Moisten the surface of the dark dough, place the light dough on top of the dark and press together lightly. Moisten the top of the light layer and with the aid of a sheet of waxed paper roll tightly into a long roll. Chill thoroughly for at least 3 hours and slice about ⅛ inch thick. Arrange on a well greased cookie sheet and bake at 375°F 9 minutes.

50 cookies

Ribbon Cookies: Use last ¼ of recipe and divide into 3 portions. Color each differently. Roll out the doughs about ⅓ inch thick, cut in 2-inch strips and stack 2 inches high alternating colors. Trim sides, press together slightly, wrap in waxed paper and chill. Slice ⅛ inch thick, arrange on a greased cookie sheet and bake at 375°F 9 minutes.

50 cookies

Berlin Wreaths

1   **cup butter**
½   **teaspoon vanilla extract**
½   **cup sugar**
2   **uncooked egg yolks**
3   **hard-cooked egg yolks, sieved**
2   **cups sifted all-purpose flour**

1. Cream butter with extract; add sugar gradually, beating until fluffy.
2. Add uncooked egg yolks, one at a time, beating thoroughly after each addition; mix in hard-cooked egg yolks.
3. Add flour in fourths, mixing until blended after each addition. Chill dough thoroughly.
4. Shape small amounts of dough into strips 4 inches long and ¼ inch thick; the ends of strips should be slightly pointed. Form wreaths on ungreased cookie sheets, overlapping ends of strips about ¼ inch.
5. Brush wreaths with slightly beaten **egg white;** sprinkle lightly with crushed **loaf sugar.**
6. Bake at 350°F 10 to 12 minutes.

About 5 dozen cookies

Lemon Angels

    Red, yellow, and green food coloring
1¾   **cups flaked coconut**
1   **cup butter**
1   **teaspoon vanilla extract**
1½   **cups sifted confectioners' sugar**
1   **egg**
2¼   **cups all-purpose flour**
½   **teaspoon baking soda**
¼   **teaspoon salt**
1   **tablespoon grated lemon peel**

1. To tint coconut, use 3 jars, one for each color. Blend 2 or 3 drops food coloring with a few drops of water in each jar. Put one-third of coconut into each jar; cover and shake vigorously until coconut is evenly tinted. Turn into shallow dishes and set aside.
2. Cream butter with vanilla extract in a bowl. Add confectioners' sugar gradually, creaming well. Add egg and beat thoroughly.
3. Blend flour, baking soda, and salt; add gradually to creamed mixture, mixing well. Stir in lemon peel.
4. Divide dough into thirds and chill until easy to handle.
5. For each third, roll teaspoonfuls of dough in one color of coconut, form balls, and place on ungreased cookie sheets.
6. Bake at 325°F 10 to 12 minutes. Remove immediately to wire racks to cool.

About 8 dozen cookies

Stone Jar Ginger Cookies

¾   **cup shortening**
1½   **cups molasses**
5   **tablespoons boiling water**
4   **cups cake flour**
2   **teaspoons soda**
¼   **teaspoon salt**
1½   **teaspoons ginger**
½   **teaspoon cinnamon**

1. Cream shortening, add molasses and water and blend.
2. Sift the dry ingredients and add to mixture.
3. The resulting dough is very soft and must be chilled overnight.
4. Roll out ⅛ inch thick on a well-floured pastry cloth. Use any shape cutter.
5. Bake at 375°F 12 minutes.

144 cookies 2-inch diameter

Desserts

Holiday Bread Pudding

3	cups milk
4	cups bread cubes (5 to 6 slices)
3	tablespoons melted butter or margarine
½	cup (3 oz.) mixed candied fruits
½	cup (about 3 oz.) golden raisins
½	cup (about 2 oz.) coarsely chopped black walnuts
10	maraschino cherries, quartered and well drained
3	eggs, slightly beaten
½	cup sugar
½	teaspoon nutmeg
½	teaspoon cinnamon
½	teaspoon allspice

1. Butter a shallow 2-qt. casserole.
2. Scald milk.
3. Meanwhile, toast bread slices until very crisp.
4. Cut toast into ½-in. cubes; put into casserole. Turning cubes lightly with a fork, drizzle over butter.
5. Add candied fruits, raisins, black walnuts, and cherries gradually and mix thoroughly with fork. Set aside.
6. Blend eggs, sugar, nutmeg, cinnamon and allspice. Add milk gradually, stirring constantly and vigorously. Pour over bread cube mixture; turn with fork to blend well.
7. Bake at 325°F 35 to 40 min., or until a metal knife comes out clean when inserted in pudding halfway between center and edge.
8. Meanwhile, prepare Custard Sauce (below).
9. Serve pudding warm with warm custard sauce and sprinkle with nutmeg.
10. Serve immediately.

7 or 8 servings

Custard Sauce: Scald **2 cups milk.** Beat 2 eggs slightly and blend in **¼ cup sugar** and **⅛ teaspoon salt.** Gradually pour milk into egg mixture, stirring vigorously at first; strain through a fine sieve into top of double boiler. Cook over boiling water, stirring constantly and rapidly, until mixture coats a metal spoon. Remove from water at once; blend in **1 teaspoon vanilla extract** and ½ **teaspoon almond extract.**

Nesselrode Pudding

8	cook chestnuts, broken in-to small pieces
	Maraschino syrup
3	cups milk
½	teaspoon salt
1½	cups sugar
5	egg yolks, beaten
2	cups heavy cream, whipped
¼	cup pineapple juice
1½	cups cooked chestnuts, pressed through a sieve
½	cup chopped candied fruit
¼	cup seedless raisins

1. Soak broken chestnut pieces overnight in maraschino syrup.
2. Scald milk in top of double boiler.
3. Beat salt, sugar and egg yolks together and add milk gradually, stirring constantly. Return to double boiler and cook until thickened, stirring constantly.
4. Strain, cool and add whipped cream, pineapple juice and chestnut puree. Turn half of mixture in mold or freezing tray of refrigerator.
5. To the remaining half, add candied fruit, raisins and broken chestnut pieces. Fill mold or tray with this mixture and freeze.
6. When firm, unmold and serve with whipped cream flavored with maraschino syrup and small pieces of cooked chestnuts.

Serves 8

Note: The maraschino syrup, pineapple juice and seedless raisins may be omitted.

Baked Apples with Red Wine

8	apples, cored
	Cherry or strawberry preserves
½	cup sugar
½	teaspoon mace or nutmeg
1	cup red wine
½	teaspoon vanilla extract

1. Place apples in a buttered casserole or baking dish. Fill each with preserves.
2. Blend sugar and mace; stir in wine and vanilla extract. Pour over apples. Cover.
3. Bake at 350°F 1 hour.
4. Chill 2 to 4 hours before serving.

8 servings

Twelve-Fruit Compote

3	cups water
1	pound mixed dried fruits including pears, figs, apricots, and peaches
1	cup pitted prunes
½	cup raisins or currants
1	cup pitted sweet cherries
2	apples, peeled and sliced or 6 ounces dried apple slices
½	cup cranberries
1	cup sugar
1	lemon, sliced
6	whole cloves
2	cinnamon sticks (3 inches each)
1	orange
½	cup grapes, pomegranate seeds, or pitted plums
½	cup fruit-flavored brandy

1. Combine water, mixed dried fruits, prunes, and raisins in a 6-quart kettle. Bring to boiling. Cover; simmer about 20 minutes, or until fruits are plump and tender.
2. Add cherries, apples, and cranberries. Stir in sugar, lemon, and spices. Cover; simmer 5 minutes.
3. Grate peel of orange; reserve. Peel and section orange, removing all skin and white membrane. Add to fruits in kettle.
4. Stir in grapes and brandy. Bring just to boiling. Remove from heat. Stir in orange peel. Cover; let stand 15 minutes.

About 12 servings

Steamed Pumpkin Pudding

1¼	cups fine dry crumbs
½	cup sifted all-purpose flour
1	cup lightly packed brown sugar
1	teaspoon baking powder
½	teaspoon baking soda
½	teaspoon salt
½	teaspoon ground cinnamon
½	teaspoon ground cloves
2	eggs, fork beaten
1½	cpus canned pumpkin
½	cup cooking or salad oil
½	cup undiluted evaporated milk
	Lemon Zest Creme

1. Combine bread crumbs, flour, brown sugar, baking powder, baking soda, salt, cinnamon, and cloves in a large bowl. Set aside.
2. Beat eggs and remaining ingredients together. Add to dry ingredients; mix until blended.
3. Turn into a well greased 1½-quart mold. Cover tightly with a greased cover, or tie greased aluminum foil tightly over mold.
4. Steam about 3 hours (see below).
5. Remove pudding from steamer and unmold onto a serving plate. Decorate the plate with drained *cinnamon-apple rings*, *whipped cream*, and *sugar cubes* soaked with *lemon extract*. Immediately ignite the sugar cubes. Accompany with a bowl of Lemon Zest Creme.

One 2¼-Pound Pudding

Lemon Zest Creme: Cream **½ cup butter or margarine** with **½ teaspoon ground ginger** and **¼ teaspoon salt** in a bowl. Add *two cups confectioners' sugar* gradually, beating constantly. Add **¼ cup lemon juice** gradually, continuing to beat until blended. Mix in **½ cup chopped nuts.**

About 2½ cups Creme

How To Steam Pudding

1. Use a mold or tin can large enough that the batter will fill mold one half to two thirds.
2. Grease the mold and the cover. If mold has no cover, use aluminum foil, parchment paper, or a double thickness of waxed paper tied on tightly.
3. Place filled mold on trivet in a steamer or deep kettle with a tight-fitting cover.
4. Pour boiling water into the steamer to no more than one half the height of the mold. Add more boiling water during the steaming period, if necessary.
5. Tightly cover steamer.
6. Keep water boiling gently at all times.
7. If pudding is to be stored several days before serving, unmold onto wire rack. Let stand until cold. Wrap in foil and store in a cool place.
8. To resteam, heat pudding in a double boiler over simmering water or set foil-wrapped pudding on a trivet in steamer over a small amount of boiling water. Steam thoroughly.

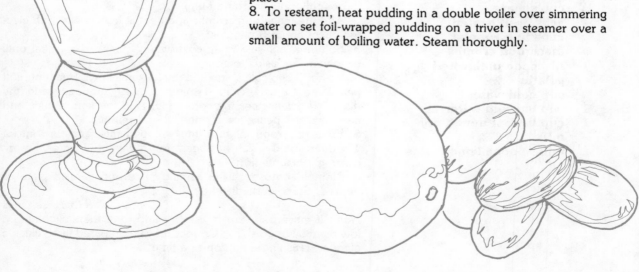

Indian Pudding

3 cups milk
½ cup yellow cornmeal
¼ cup sugar
1 teaspoon salt
1 teaspoon ground cin-
    namon
½ teaspoon ground ginger
1 egg, well beaten
½ cup molasses
2 tablespoons butter
1 cup cold milk

1. Scald the 3 cups milk in the top of a double boiler. Stirring constantly, slowly blend into milk a mixture of the cornmeal, sugar, salt, cinnamon, and ginger. Stir in a blend of the egg of molasses.
2. Cook and stir over boiling water 10 minutes, or until very thick. Beat in the butter.
3. Turn into a well-buttered 1½-quart casserole. Pour cold milk over top.
4. Bake at 300°F 2 hours, or until browned.

About 6 servings

Chocolate-Mocha Cream Pudding

2 ounces (2 squares)
    unsweetened chocolate
1 cup double-strength coffee
⅔ cup sugar
¼ cup flour
¼ teaspoon salt
1 cup milk
3 egg yolks, slightly beaten
2 tablespoons butter or
    margarine
2 teaspoons vanilla extract

1. Heat chocolate and coffee together over low heat until chocolate is melted; stir to blend.
2. Meanwhile, combine the sugar, flour, and salt in top of a double boiler. Blend in milk.
3. Add the hot coffee-chocolate mixture gradually, stirring until blended. Continue to stir and bring rapidly to boiling; boil 2 minutes.
4. Stir a small amount of hot mixture into the egg yolks. Immediately blend into mixture in double boiler. Cook over simmering water 5 minutes; stir to keep it cooking evenly.
5. Remove from simmering water and blend in butter and vanilla extract. Chill thoroughly before serving.

4 to 6 servings

Macaroon Mousse

½ cup butter or margarine
1 teaspoon vanilla extract
¾ cup sugar
4 eggs, well beaten
1¾ cups fine almond
    macaroon crumbs
1 teaspoon unflavored
    gelatin
¼ cup cold water
1 cup icy cold water
1 cup instant nonfat dry
    milk
2 tablespoons lemon juice

1. Cream butter with extract until softened. Gradually beat in the sugar until thoroughly blended. Add the eggs in thirds, beating thoroughly until light and fluffy.
2. Add the macaroon crumbs and beat at high speed with electric mixer about 5 minutes.
3. Soften gelatin in ¼ cup cold water. Stir over low heat until dissolved. Set aside to cool.
4. Mix the 1 cup cold water and dry milk in a bowl. Beat until soft peaks are formed, 3 to 4 minutes. Very gradually add the dissolved gelatin, beating constantly. Add the lemon juice and beat until stiff peaks are formed, 3 to 4 minutes.
5. Fold macaroon mixture into whipped milk and turn into a 1½-quart mold which has been rinsed with cold water. Freeze overnight or until firm.
6. Unmold onto a chilled serving plate and garnish plate as desired. Serve immediately.

8 to 10 servings

Note: If macaroons are moist, dry and toast them slightly in a low oven befor crushing. Crumbs may be prepared in an electric blender, crushing a portion at a time.

Pots de Creme Chocolat

2   cups whipping cream
1   tablespoon sugar
4   ounces sweet chocolate, melted
6   egg yolks, beaten
1½   teaspoons vanilla extract

1. Heat the cream and sugar together in the top of a double boiler over simmering water until cream is scalded. Add the melted chocolate and stir until blended. Pour mixture into beaten egg yolks, beating constantly until blended. Stir in vanilla extract.
2. Strain through a fine sieve into 8 small earthenware pots or custard cups. Set pots in a pan of hot water.
3. Bake at 325°F 20 minutes. (Mixture will become thicker upon cooling.)
4. Set cups on wire rack to cool; chill thoroughly.

8 servings

Christmas Squares

Almond Paste
1½   cups ground almonds
1⅔   cups confectioners' sugar
2   egg whites

2   oz. candied cherries
2   oz. candied orange peel
2   oz. candied lemon peel
4   oz. semi-sweet chocolate
2   oz. coconut flakes

1. Make almond paste. Mix ground almonds and confectioners' sugar, then add egg whites and blend until smooth. Mix in candied fruit.
2. Roll out almond paste to a stick. Flatten it on four sides so that each side is about 2″. Chill.
3. Cut the stick into slices. Melt the chocolate over a double boiler and brush on the slices. Sprinkle the coconut flakes on top. Chill again.

Christmas Balls

3   cups almond paste (see Christmas Squares)
2   lbs. almonds
1   box paper candy cups
6   oz. semi-sweet chocolate

1. Work almond paste until smooth. Roll paste in small balls and work a whole almond into the center of each. Place in paper candy cups.
2. Melt chocolate in the top of a double boiler and pour 1 tbs. over each cut. Let them set.

A variation is to divide the almond paste into 3 parts. Mix yellow, red and green food coloring into the almond paste. Roll into small balls and place in paper cups. Decorate with hazelnuts or walnuts.

Beverages

Hot Buttered Cranberry Punch

1½   cups water
⅔   cup firmly packed brown sugar
½   teaspoon cinnamon
¼   teaspoon allspice
⅛   teaspoon cloves
⅛   teaspoon nutmeg
⅛   teaspoon salt
1   can (18 ounces) unsweetened pineapple juice
2   cups water
4   cups fresh cranberries, rinsed and sorted
    Butter or margarine

1. Combine 1½ cups water, brown sugar, spices, and salt in a saucepan. Bring to boiling. Reduce heat and simmer 5 minutes.
2. Transfer mixture to an electric cooker. Add pineapple juice.
3. Cover and cook on Low 2 hours.
4. Meanwhile, bring 2 cups water to boiling in a saucepan. Add cranberries and cook, uncovered, until the skins pop.
5. Force cranberries through a food mill or sieve to make a puree. Stir puree into mixture in electric cooker.
6. Cover and ook on Low 15 to 30 minutes to combine flavors.
7. Ladle punch into serving cups or mugs and add dots of butter to each cup. Serve with cinnamon stick stirrers, if desired.

About 1½ quarts punch

Spicy Cranberry Punch

4   pieces (3 in. each) stick cinnamon, broken in pieces
8   whole allspice
18   whole cloves
3   qts. cranberry juice cocktail
1   orange, sliced
6   bottles (7 oz. each) lemon-lime carbonated beverage, chilled

1. Tie spices together in cheesecloth bag.
2. In a large saucepan, combine the cranberry juice cocktail, orange slices, and spice bag. Bring to boiling, reduce heat, and simmer about 20 minutes. Set aside to cool; discard spice bag and orange; chill cranberry juice.
3. Just before serving, pour into chilled punch bowl; add lemon-lime carbonated beverage and stir to blend. If desired, garnish with additional *orange slices*.

About 17 cups

Egg Nog

1 egg, beaten
1 tablespoon sugar or honey
   Salt
¾ cup milk
¼ teaspoon vanilla
   Dash nutmeg

1. Combine egg with sugar and salt, add milk and vanilla.
2. Serve cold in tall glasses and sprinkle with nutmeg.
3. For a fluffy eggnog separate egg, beat white until stiff, then fold into egg yolk mixture.
4. May be served hot or cold, for 1.

Mulled Cider

2 quarts sweet apple cider
20 whole cloves
½ cup sugar
12 sticks cinnamon
14 whole allspice
¼ teaspoon salt

1. Combine ingredients in the order listed.
2. Heat to boiling and simmer 15 minutes.
3. Allow to stand 12 hours.
4. Strain and serve hot.

Serves 8 to 10

Hot Spiced Cider

2 quarts apple cider
⅓ cup lightly packed brown sugar
2 sticks cinnamon
1 teaspoon whole cloves
1 teaspoon whole allspice

1. Put ingredients into an electric cooker; stir to mix thoroughly.
2. Cover and cook on Low 2 hours, or until as hot as desired.
3. Serve in hot mugs.

About 2 quarts spiced cider

Greek Coffee

1 heaping teaspoon Greek coffee*
½ teaspoon sugar
1 demitasse cup filled almost to the brim with water

1. Place coffee and sugar in a Greek coffeepot, a briki, or a narrow saucepot. Add the water and stir until well blended.
2. Place coffee pot on low heat and wait for coffee to boil. Remove from heat. Let coffee simmer down. Return to heat. Allow to reach boiling again. Remove from heat.
3. With a spoon skim a little of the foam, called "kamaki," off the top and gently place it in the bottom of the cup. Slowly pour the coffee into the cup, being careful not to disturb the kamaki.

*Greek and Turkish coffee are the same.

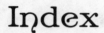

Index